THE JUDGMENT OF THE GODS

AND OTHER VERDICTS OF HISTORY

ROBERT REGINALD

THE BORGO PRESS

MMXI

THE JUDGMENT OF THE GODS

Copyright © 1998, 2001, 2002, 2005, 2011 by Robert Reginald
[p. 9 shall constitute an extension of this copyright page]

FIRST EDITION

Published by Wildside Press LLC

www.wildsidebooks.com

DEDICATION

For My Dear Mother,

Betty Burgess,

A Mystery in Her Own Right

CONTENTS

Acknowledgments 9

Introduction: The Verdict of History 11

The Judgment of the Gods 15

Occam's Razor 41

Occam's Treasure 65

Occam's Measure 93

About the Author 123

ACKNOWLEDGMENTS

THESE STORIES WERE previously published as follows, and are reprinted (with some editing, updating, and textual modifications) by permission of the author:

"The Judgment of the Gods" first appeared as "The Judgement of the Gods," in *The Mammoth Book of Historical Whodunnits, Third New Collection*, edited by Mike Ashley (London: Robinson, 2005), and simultaneously as "The Judgment of the Gods" in *The Mammoth Book of New Historical Whodunits*, edited by Mike Ashley (New York: Carroll & Graf, 2005). Copyright © 2005, 2011 by Robert Reginald.

"Occam's Razor" first appeared in *On Crusade: More Tales of the Knights Templar*, edited by Katherine Kurtz (New York: Warner Books, 1998 & 2003), and was reprinted, with changes, in *Katydid & Other Critters: Tales of Fantasy and Mystery*, by Robert Reginald (Riverside, Calif.: Ariadne Press, 2001). Copyright © 1998, 2001, 2011 by Robert Reginald.

"Occam's Treasure" first appeared in *Crusade of Fire: Mystical Tales of the Knights Templar*, edited by Katherine Kurtz (New York: Warner Books, 2002). Copyright © 2002, 2011 by Robert Reginald.

"Occam's Measure" is published here for the first time. Copyright © 2011 by Robert Reginald.

INTRODUCTION
THE VERDICT OF HISTORY

I DON'T WRITE many short works of fiction. I find longer lengths more attractive, more salable, and more interesting, so there's never been much impetus on my part to produce such tales.

Still, over the course of a four-decade-plus career as a professional wordmonger and editor, I've written and sold a score of fictions less than 30,000 words in length. The first three pieces in this collection were commissioned by the editors, and written to the requirements of the markets in question. So the first two William of Occam tales, "Occam's Razor" and "Occam's Treasure," for example, include the Knights Templar as a major element of each story, since it was the central theme of those two anthologies. I couldn't have written them in any other way and maintained the sale.

The third adventure of William and his sidekick, Brother Thaddæus, "Occam's Measure," was partially outlined a decade ago, when I was anticipating making a series of these stories; and then resurrected and written specifically for this collection. I wanted to have the great thinker forced to confront the female of the species—and also to face the truly awful things that have been done to both men and women in the name of politics, religion, or just plain evil.

William of Occam made an excellent detective. Once I'd done the research on the period in which he lived, I found a rich stew of philosophical and political strife in which to frame his investigations. His championship of the principle known today as "Occam's Razor" also suggested to me that he had the ability to see through the pretensions of others, and to discern the strands of truth in a muddled criminous puzzle.

His "boss," Pope John XXII, provided me with a slimy villain whose ruthlessness was well documented. The former Cardinal Duèse had survived French King Philip IV's machinations and the fall of the Templars, only to be elected as a compromise "interim" pontiff after the death of Pope Clement V. Instead, he wound up confounding, outliving, and outmaneuvering most of his enemies. Nobody much liked John, but no one ever discounted him, either.

At one point I also outlined and started a novel featuring William of Occam, *The White Death*, plus several sequels. These passages still survive, but whether I'll have the time or energy to accomplish that work remains to be seen.

* * * * * * *

THE FOURTH STORY, "The Judgment of the Gods," was written for fellow bibliographer, editor, and historian Mike Ashley. The murder of King Sennacherib of Assyria remains a bona fide mystery of history. The official Assyrian annals of the state carefully obscure the circumstances of his passing in 681 BCE, and the succession of a younger son, King Esarhaddon. Indeed, we only know of the crime because of a passage in the Bible and corroborating evidence in the *Babylonian Chronicle*.

I inserted a young, objective outside observer into the mix, a trader from western Asia Minor who's the grandson of the poet Homer. I spent three years in Izmir (the ancient Greek city Zmyrna—later Smyrna) in my youth, and I was generally familiar with the area and its history; and I'd also delved fairly extensively into the culture and language of the Assyrian and Babylonian Empires.

Of course, no one knows where Homer was born, although a number of ancient cities, many of them in Asia Minor, claimed the honor. My intent was to have my young merchant detective, Achilleus, live through a series of criminous adventures in Nineveh, and then witness the destruction of that city first-hand in his old age—in 612 BCE. Maybe I'll yet get around to penning those tales!

For now, gentle readers, I hope you enjoy these four stories of the past-made-present-made-future.

Blessèd be!

—Robert Reginald
San Bernardino, California
9 July and 20 October 2010

THE JUDGMENT OF THE GODS

NINEVEH, CAPITAL OF ASSYRIA
*Twentieth Day of Tebetu, in the
Year Named for the Eponym Nabu-Sharru-Usur
(January, 681 BC)*

THE GREAT KING Sennacherib lay prostrate before the altar of the god, his face pressed to the cold tile floor, his arms outstretched in supplication towards the huge, flickering image of the eagle-headed deity looming above him. Torches mounted in alcoves on either side of the small hall provided minimal light.

"My relatives plot against me," he murmured. "My enemies are legion. I have destroyed the city of Babylon to avenge the death of my eldest son, but those whom I let live now wish my death. Everywhere I see war and plague and famine. When shall it end? When shall the burden pass from my hands?"

A sudden breath of winter air pressed the robe against his legs. He shivered in spite of himself. A moan seemed to emanate from the mouth of the god.

"What did you say?" the Great King said. "Tell me what to do."

A second groan echoed through the chamber. The guard captain standing just inside the door at the other end of the hall woke from his reverie at the noise, peering into the darkness.

Suddenly and quite without warning, the vast statue of the deity tipped forward and fell directly onto the king.

The guard screamed a cry of warning, echoed by the troop posted outside. But it was too late. As he could quite clearly see when he rushed to his master's aid, Sennacherib, the Great King, the Mighty King, the King of the Four Corners of the World, was quite, quite dead.

"The judgment of the gods!" the captain said, as the other soldiers rushed to his side. "The gods have spoken!"

And so they had.

* * * * * * *

ACHILLEUS OF ZMYRNA in Asia Minor sends greetings to his father's father in Chios. May the son of Meles sing a thousand more songs before he rests!

In the third year of the twenty-fourth Olympiad, I accompanied the expedition of your son Telemachos to Assyria, there to establish a regular system of trade with the Great King Sennacherib and his ministers, now that their hegemony extended to the shores of the Mediterranean Sea. By your instruction I had learned the art and science of lettering from the Phoenician merchants of Akko who were wont to visit our fair harbor, and this skill, it was thought, might give our party some small edge in the bargaining yet to come.

We were three months on our journey, first by ship around the coast of Anatolia, and thence overland up the Orontes and across the great waste to Mesopotamia. When we finally arrived in the walled city of Nineveh, not long after the close of summer, we were thoroughly tired of traveling and ready to meet with the king and his officials.

This proved, however, somewhat more difficult than we had imagined.

These "Black-Haired Men," as they call themselves, are a strange folk indeed. They speak a tongue akin to Phoenician, yet etch their scratchings upon tablets of clay, like the tracks of birds upon the beach. Not even their rulers can read the inscriptions engraved upon their own monuments. They welcome the settlement of strangers within their chief citadels, so that their own people have become a minority in some of their cities, and promote such individuals to the highest levels of service in their government, but force them to bow and scrape as if they were no better than slaves. I do not understand how any man can tolerate such treatment.

We sent our embassies to various high officials, but none would receive us. We sought out the major trading companies in the city, but while all treated us courteously, none would treat with us without the approval of the government. Thus matters rested while fall advanced into winter.

I had been directed by Uncle Telemachos to acquire as much of their language as quickly as possible, and so I sought out one of the Houses of Scribes, a place where youths were regularly initiated into the mysteries of the stylus and the clay tablet. I asked the Headmaster if I could participate, even though I was older than most of these boys. A contribution to the god eased my passage immeasurably.

The study was most difficult. It was as if these men had purposely designed a system that would be impossible for the average citizen to learn, which was perhaps the whole point of the exercise. Scribes are highly valued for their services here, being among the best paid members of society.

I befriended an older lad named Asarbaniplos, which is the closest I can render his name in the Greek tongue. I understood at the time that he was related to the chief families of the city, but exactly how, I did not know. Assyrians do not talk about such matters. I never learned, for example, how old he was, for the year of one's birth is a closely held secret for these people.

No one even knows the age of the Great King who rules them.

This "Banu," as he was commonly known, had dark curly hair and a quick spirit that instinctively grasped that which seemed so elusive to me. We became great comrades in our battles over the meaning of the elusive stone tablets.

After four months' residence in the citadel, Uncle obtained an interview with the Second Vizier, during which he asked to see the Great King. He was laughed out of the palace. "No man may talk with the emissary of the gods," he was told.

Several days later I was studying in the House of Scribes when a commotion interrupted our lesson.

"What's happening?" I asked.

"The Great King is dead," my friend said. He shook his bushy head, unable to comprehend what he was saying. "The gods have struck him down. They have cursed Assyria." Then he ran out the door, not heeding my shouts to stop.

I returned to our apartment, and we stayed close to home the next few weeks. The streets were filled with thieves and rogues eager to steal money, food, even the clothing off one's back. Finally, order was restored by two of the old king's sons, one of whom was proclaimed his successor. Still, the evident dissatisfaction of the people was everywhere apparent.

When another month had passed, we heard of an army approaching from the west. Crown Prince Esarhaddon had gathered together his forces and was marching on the capital. The Substitute King went out to meet him, but was defeated and reportedly fled.

A few days later, a squad of guards knocked on our door, and ordered Uncle Telemachos and me to accompany them. We marched out of the Hatamti Gate, where we mounted horses and headed northeast onto the open plain. We could see our breaths blowing behind us upon the wind.

"Where are we going?" I asked.

"Speak when you are spoken to," the guard said, emphasizing the point with a wave of his spear. I dutifully obeyed.

We rode until we spied a citadel, which I later learned was

called Fort Sargon. We dismounted and the guard blindfolded us.

"Do not remove these on pain of death," he said.

Then they took Uncle and myself by the elbow, and guided us through a series of long, echoing passageways paved with stone.

Finally, we entered a large hall, judging by the change in sound, where we were both forced to the ground, prostrated upon the cold floor. We heard the tramp, tramp, tramp of a squad of soldiers coming through a doorway and across the room. Our "gentle" companions raised us to our knees.

"What are your names?" came the harsh inquiry.

"What is he saying?" Uncle asked.

"We are Telemachos and Achilleus, traders from Zmyrna," I said.

"Te-le-ma-khu," the hidden man stuttered. "A-khu-i-lai," he added. "These are hard for the Black-Haired Men to say." He paused. "Why does your senior not speak for himself?"

"He does not understand your language," I said. "No disrespect was intended."

"Then you may become his voice," he said. "Tell him what I have said and what I will say, and translate his responses for me, exactly as he gives them. Do you understand?"

"I do, sir," I said, turning my head slightly so Uncle could hear, and relating what I had been told thus far.

"Who is this man? What does he want?" Telemachos asked.

I repeated these questions in Akkadian.

One of the guards struck me down with his spear.

"Enough!" he said. "Withdraw, all of you."

"But, sir...."

"Let them be seated. Then leave us."

The stools were unpadded, but they were immeasurably easier on our limbs than that tile floor had been.

"I am Ashur-Akhi-Iddina, son of Sin-Akhe-Eriba," the voice intoned, a hint of pride floating upon the air.

I sat suddenly upright.

"The Great King!" I hissed to Uncle.

THE JUDGMENT OF THE GODS | 19

"What?" he said.

"Esarhaddon! The new king!" I said again between clenched lips.

"Yes," came the reply, "by right of succession and by conquest, but not legally until I enter the walls of Nineveh, which I must do soon, on a day and at an hour that the priests deem propitious.

"But I have a difficulty. My glorious father, contrary to popular report, was murdered. I have questioned my two rebellious brothers most vigorously (they did not escape!), but they deny any complicity in the death of their sire. I believe them. Someone else in my father's court was responsible for his death, and I need to know who it is before I enter upon my patrimony.

"My son says that you Greeks have a strong sense of justice, and have been trained to discern fact from fiction. He also tells me that you desire to establish trade between your city and our empire. Therefore, we each have something to gain from the bargain.

"I give you seven days to find the culprit, no more. If you are unable to do so, you may depart in peace, but thereafter we will see no more of you within the boundaries of our kingdom, upon pain of death. If you succeed, you will have our blessing upon your enterprise."

All the while I was translating his words for Uncle Telemachos, who paused before replying with my voice.

"O great and mighty king," he said, "we are simple merchants, with no experience of crime beyond that of ordinary citizens, but we will do what we can to help. We will need the assistance of one of your men as intermediary, and will also require your authority to enter into any place at any time to question any person."

I do not think that the Great King was overly pleased with Uncle's reply, but he finally said: "My son will accompany you." Then: "This interview is over." He clapped his hands three times to call his guards.

We were escorted from the building and back to our horses,

where we could feel the warmth of the winter sun, Great Eos, shining down upon us once again. When our blindfolds were removed, the first person I saw was my friend, Banu.

"What are you doing here?" I asked.

"*I* am the son," came the simple reply, and suddenly much that was murky became very clear to me.

* * * * * * *

THE NEXT DAY we held a council of war, and Uncle expressed reservations over what we might accomplish.

"Will not the Great King kill us if we fail this task?" he asked. I translated this.

"Father will not break his word," Banu said.

"Who can help us while being discrete?" I asked Banu.

"My *Turtanu*," the lad said. When I expressed some puzzlement over the word, he elaborated: "Erishum is my, well, you might call him my chief 'officer.' He manages my household and provides security and anything else I need."

"I was not previously aware of his presence," I said.

"That was deliberate," came the reply, "but he *is* trustworthy."

Uncle Telemachos said: "We must see the place where the crime took place."

"The temple has been sealed since my grandfather's death," Banu said. He clapped his hands once, and a short, bearded man appeared at the doorway. He was armed with a long knife or short spear. "Erishum," the prince said, and the man bowed. He sent the *Turtanu* to fetch the guards who would open the way for us.

We soon set out for the House of Nisroch, the god of wisdom. I had not previously heard his name, and so indicated to Banu.

"He is called Marduk in the south," Banu said, "being reckoned there as king of the gods of Babylon."

"But not here," I said.

"Here Ashur is king," he said. "That is why Nisroch dwells in such a small house."

The temple was a square building near the Halzi Gate, decorated with the huge images of winged bulls pacing around the outside walls. A troop of soldiers flanked the sole entrance. They came to attention when they spied the prince approaching.

Banu presented the stone cylinder of his father's authority to the officer on duty, who identified himself as Captain Azizu. The prince had specifically asked for him to be present.

Azizu broke the clay seal linking the two massive cedar doors, and pushed them open. His guards rushed in to light the torches flanking either side of the hall.

My first impression was of the shifting images of a herd of great beasts ready to devour us if we stepped inside. Lining the inside of the structure were the images of the Assyrian gods and goddesses, culminating in the toppled stone statue at the other end.

"You were in charge that day?" the prince asked.

"I was," the officer said.

"Tell us about your procedure," Banu said.

"Whenever the Great King wished to talk with the god," Azizu said, "I or Captain Ukin-Zer would gather a squad of thirty men, whoever happened to be on duty at the time, and would proceed to the temple. There the Great King would wait outside while I and ten others searched the interior of the hall, clearing out anyone who might remain. Usually, the Great King visited during my night watch, after his appointments had been completed, when no one else was present."

"And that night?" the prince said.

"We found no one. After my men had cleared the changing rooms at the rear of the hall, I searched them again before allowing the Great King to enter. Then I stood duty just inside the entrance, as I always do, so that he was never left unattended."

"No one was there?" Uncle asked.

"No one," he said. "I swear. The temple was deserted."

"Then what happened?" Banu asked.

"The god toppled over on him without warning. I could do

nothing, although I rushed to help as soon as I saw what was happening. When I reached the Great King, he was already dead, crushed beneath the stone. We removed the body, as required, but everything else was left as you see it now."

"Did you search the hall again?" I asked.

"Twice again we searched the rooms and the statues and the alcoves. No one was there. *No one!*"

This was very puzzling. Now Uncle led us into the interior, directing me to take notes of everything that we saw. Banu and Azizu and Erishum followed, the others remaining outside. We searched each of the rooms in turn before returning to the main statue.

The image of the eagle-headed god Nisroch had been partially shattered by its impact with the tile floor and the Great King's body. The face and wings of the god were separated a small distance from the rest. We saw a dark stain upon the stones where the Great King's life blood had flowed across the floor. Uncle knelt by the base of the statue and examined it closely. He took out a short knife, and probed slowly around the edges.

"Look here!" he suddenly exclaimed.

We gathered 'round. There were indications of tampering, both at the front and at the rear of the base, and signs that some of the alterations had been patched over with a light veneer of plaster.

"This was no accident," he said. "This work was accomplished over a long period of time."

Someone must have known of the Great King's nocturnal habits, and planned accordingly.

"But how?" Azizu asked. "We searched the temple thoroughly, before and after. Even if someone had undermined the statue, how could it have been toppled at just the right moment to kill the Great King?"

"We must look at the underlying motives to help discover the answer to that question," Uncle said. "Who stood to gain? We should talk first with the rebel princes."

"My father will not approve," the prince said.

THE JUDGMENT OF THE GODS | 23

"If the Great King wants us to solve the unsolvable, then he must bear with us," Telemachos said. I was very proud then of your son, grandsire. He demonstrated why the sons of Meles are renowned throughout the Mediterranean for their vigor and intelligence.

Banu looked at the spot where his grandfather had perished. "I will see what I can arrange," he finally said. "But I can promise nothing."

* * * * * * *

THE NEXT MORNING, however, Banu appeared at our apartment in the city with his *Turtanu* to tell us that an interview with the two rebels had been arranged. We exited the city once again, and rode for an hour until we came to a fort constructed out of mud bricks. We were led to a small, squat, windowless building in the compound.

The guards conducted us to a room empty save for a table and stools. The first prisoner was brought to us.

"This is the high and mighty Prince Arda-Mulishi," Banu said, "he who once called himself Great King of Assyria." He spat on the ground and made a sign which I later learned was a curse, but the prisoner never reacted.

Indeed, it was clear that the man had been greatly abused. His eyes were puffy and dull, his limbs bruised, his spirit largely broken. His once fine clothes were tattered and stained with blood and dust.

Telemachos, speaking through me: "Did you kill the Great King?"

Prisoner, finally looking up: "Who are *you*, stranger, to question a prince of Assyria?"

Uncle: "I speak in the name of the Great King."

Banu slipped his father's seal from around his neck; it was tied to a cord threaded through a hole that pierced the green stone. He displayed it in his open palm.

Prisoner, glancing at Banu: "Spawn of that foreign bitch,

Naqi'a!" It was his turn to spit and laugh. The *Turtanu* struck the rebel on his back with the blunt end of his spear, sending him to his knees.

"I see you share your father's winning ways, boy," Arda-Mulishi said. Erishum raised his weapon again, but Banu held up his hand.

"Half-uncle," the prince said, "you may make this day difficult for yourself or not, as you choose. But you *will* answer."

Prisoner, still smirking: "What was the question?"

Telemachos: "Did you kill your father?"

Then the rebel prince turned to Uncle for the first time, looking him straight in the eye.

"No," he said. I did not need to translate.

Telemachos: "Do you know who did?"

"No."

Banu: "Why did you make yourself Great King in contravention of your father's will?"

Arda-Mulishi said nothing for a very long time, and then sighed: "When the Great King died at the hand of the god whom he had dispossessed from his rightful place in Babylon, the people of Assyria knew that the gods had turned against them.

"All of you who were there know of the turmoil of those days. The state was in danger of collapsing. Esarhaddon was far away in Armenia.

"The Great King Sennacherib told me the month before his passing that I would be restored to my rightful place in the House of Succession on New Year's Day, two months hence. I was his eldest surviving son after my senior brother, King Ashur-Nadin-Shumi, whom the Babylonians sold to the Elamites twelve years ago. My mother was First Queen to the Great King. She was Assyrian, not Phoenician. She kept her own name, and did not have to change it to something else.

"This was my birthright once, and would have been again, and so I seized what was mine. But I failed to consult with the gods, and the gods were still angry with Assyria. The real killer betrayed me, whomever that person was. I could never find out,

THE JUDGMENT OF THE GODS | 25

although I tried. There was no time to continue in the midst of crisis."

Telemachos: "You investigated the death of your father? How?"

Arda-Mulishi: "I ordered the *Turtanu* who saw the murder, Captain Azizu, to interrogate those who were likely to benefit from my father's death."

Telemachos: "What did he report?"

Arda-Mulishi: "He had no time to report. Shortly thereafter, I had to join the forces being assembled to meet Esarhaddon's advancing army, and I never saw Captain Azizu again."

That was all he would say. I later learned that he had been executed not long thereafter.

We next interrogated another son of the deceased Great King, Prince Nabu-Sharru-Usur, who had supported his brother's rebellion, and for whom the present year had been named. The difference in appearance between the two men was striking. Nabu was clean and well-dressed and had not been abused. I raised an eyebrow at my young friend.

"He has to present my father to the gods when he takes his rightful place upon the throne," Banu said. "He still has a role to play."

Nabu-Sharru-Usur: "Yes, I do." His voice was high and thin, like a woman's, and I suddenly realized that this was a man who would never have to shave again.

He gathered his robes about him, and sat down on a stool with a sigh. "Get on with it," he said.

Telemachos: "Did you conspire to kill the Great King?"

Nabu-Sharru-Usur: "He was my father. He made a place for me among the highest nobles of the land. You see what I am. I could never be the Great King because of that. I had a good place at court, a life of beauty and luxury and power. Why would I give that up?"

Telemachos: "For greater power?"

Nabu-Sharru-Usur: "What greater power? Already I had the Great King's confidence. Already I lived as I pleased. There was nothing else I wanted. Because of his death, all of that is gone. I must play my little role for my half-brother, and then exit history. Isn't that true, nephew?" He looked down at Prince Banu.

Banu: "I wouldn't know."

Telemachos: "Who murdered your father?"

Nabu-Sharru-Usur: "One of those Babylonian scum. We did everything for them, and do you think they were grateful? Not a bit. Always complaining, always moaning about this and that. Yes, one of the Babylonians killed him. I have no doubt whatever. They all hated him for razing their city."

Telemachos: "Your brother said he was about to be renamed Crown Prince."

Nabu-Sharru-Usur: "Everyone knew that my father had changed his mind again about the succession. It was Nisroch, you see. The god told him that he needed to make amends for stealing the deity from his ancestral home. Mortal man may not interfere with the immortal gods. Nisroch wanted to be Marduk again. He would not be propitiated. Father refused, and the god killed him."

Telemachos: "The statue was tampered with. A man killed the Great King."

Nabu-Sharru-Usur: "The gods work through men to achieve their ends. It was the judgment of the gods."

We learned nothing else from him.

Later over dinner, we talked about our next step.

"We must locate one or more of the guards who were on duty that day," Uncle said.

"Why?" I asked. "We've already talked to Captain Azizu."

"Yes, but having a different view of the same event might help us discover what actually occurred. Also, we should interview Queen Naqi'a."

Prince Banu did not think the latter would be possible, but agreed to inquire about the guards.

That was the end of the second day.

THE JUDGMENT OF THE GODS | 27

* * * * * * *

THE NEXT MORNING was cold and drizzly, but we felt we were making good progress, at least until the young prince appeared.

"They're all gone!" Banu said as he entered our apartment.

"Who?" I asked.

"The guards who were on duty that night. They were all sent to the army shortly thereafter, and have not returned. Most are probably dead. However, I found a friend of one of the sergeants, and he may be able to tell us something."

This was Sergeant Iqisu, a rough-hewed man in his forties, waiting just outside our door. We brought him in.

The prince took the lead: "You knew Sergeant Yari?"

"I did," came the reply. "We trained together years ago, and we were assigned to the same squads throughout our careers."

"Tell us what he said about the Great King's death."

"Well, prince"—he bowed at each of us in turn—"it was all passing strange. A half-month before the, uh, incident, Cap'n Azizu brought in a bunch of new recruits, really green under the gills, if you know what I mean, and gave them to Sergeants Yari and Banba to train. Yari complained about it at the time. These rubes just didn't know one end of the spear from the other. They had to be taught everything. Usually, we get only the best. But they didn't even ken much Akkadian."

"Did the guards follow their usual procedure that evening?" I said, translating Uncle's words.

"Yes, sir," Iqisu said. "Yari said they searched the place quite thoroughly, as usual, and found no one there, before or after."

"Can you normally see inside the temple when the Great King is present?"

"No, sir. The doors are partially kept shut to give him space to talk with his god. Only the officer remains to watch over the Great King."

"What about the captain?" I asked. "Is he visible?"

"Those of us stationed near the front of the temple can often glimpse his back, but we're usually watching for danger outside,

28 | ROBERT REGINALD

if you know what I mean. It's curious, though: Yari said he called to the cap'n once for assistance, when a drunk tried to enter the temple, and it took him a moment or two to respond."

"What happened to the squad who was on duty that night?" Uncle asked.

"Two days after the Great King's death, they were all drafted into the army. Men were being pulled from around the city to help face the threat from the northwest."

"Were any of your other guards reassigned?"

Iqisu shook his head "no."

Later that day, we talked about the most recent developments.

"Who *is* this Azizu?" Uncle asked.

"I have no idea," the prince said.

Erishum thought that Azizu came from somewhere in the west, but knew little else about him. "I will ask around," he said.

"How does one become an officer of the guard?" Telemachos asked.

"Such appointments are always political," the prince said. "One must have a patron in high places."

"Then who was Azizu's sponsor?"

"I do not know," Banu said.

"One thing that I do know," Uncle said, "is that all large enterprises keep very detailed records of such appointments. Where would such listings be found, Prince Banu?"

"In the House of Archives," he said, sitting up straight. "Yes, it would be there." He smiled. "I knew there was a reason that Father wanted me to learn the stylus."

"Then, if I may be so bold, my prince, I suggest that you and Achilleus spend tomorrow morning examining those files."

That was the third day.

* * * * * * *

THE HOUSE OF ARCHIVES was a nondescript structure of brick and stone near the Handuri Gate in the southern part of Nineveh. Although the prince and I had no problem entering the building, finding what we wanted proved no easy task.

"Well, yes," the librarian said, "there are filing marks on the boxes, but you would need to have one of the scribes show you the meaning of both them and the texts, and we have none available to spare for a tour."

"I can read the signs perfectly well myself," Banu said, "and I represent the Great King's interest in this, so either cooperate or you'll find yourself copying eponym lists somewhere in Outer Armenia."

"Of course, Great Prince."

"We are looking for the record of an officer's appointment."

"When did this occur?" the librarian asked.

"I have no idea," came the reply.

"Then how do you expect me?...uh, yes, I'll do everything I can," the man said, when he saw the anger building in Banu's eyes. "Where's he stationed?"

"He's part of the Great King's personal guard," the prince said. "His name is Azizu."

"Oh! Well, that should be relatively easy. He'll be recorded on the payroll of the Great King's own household. Let's just see," and the librarian went bustling off into the next room, looking at this box of tablets and that, reading the labels affixed in clay to each. "Yes, this may tell us something." He motioned to one of his orderlies to lift down the heavy container.

"Azizu, Aaa-ziii-zuuu. Aha! Says he was appointed in the eponymate of King Sennacherib himself, five years ago. This number"—he pointed at the leading edge—"tells me the location of his enrollment tablet."

The librarian ran into an adjoining storage area, and then into another further on. He had the orderly lift the heavy box onto a sorting table. Then he paged through the tablets, one by one.

"Yes, here it is. Azizu. Native of Qarqara in the west. Enlisted eleven years ago. Raised to officer rank by the Great King five years ago, on the recommendation of Queen Zakutu."

"Grandmama!" Banu exclaimed.

"But I thought her name was Naqi'a," I said.

"That was her original name. Her royal name, her Akkadian name, is Zakutu, 'the lady who was freed'."

Banu suddenly noticed the librarian's interest in their conversation, and abruptly dismissed him, saying, "You will be silent, clerk, about all of these matters, or you will lose the ability to speak and write." Then he said to me: "We'll talk of this later."

But after we had returned to our apartment, the prince brooded within himself, and finally he made his excuses and left. Only I remained to tell Uncle what had transpired.

* * * * * * *

ON THE FIFTH day we were interrupted by the appearance of Captain Azizu in our doorway.

"I hear you've been asking questions about me," he said.

"We are asking questions of many people," Uncle replied through me. "The innocent have nothing to fear."

"I just did my duty," the officer said. "Everyone who was there will confirm my account."

"Well, that's the problem, isn't it?" Telemachos said. "We have only your rendition of what occurred, because we cannot locate any of the other guards who were on duty that night. Where is Sergeant Yari, for example?"

"I have no idea, sir," Azizu said. "He was reassigned by order of the Substitute King, and I've not seen him since. He was in the army that the usurper took to Hani-Galbat. Many of those men have never returned."

"How convenient," Uncle said. "What of the rest?"

"Most of them I didn't know," the Captain said.

"Who assigned them to you?"

"Don't know that either. I am accustomed to following my orders as presented to me, sir. I do not question orders, ever. I do my job. I do it well. No one has ever questioned my efficiency. The Great King himself has praised me."

"You were ordered by the Substitute King to conduct an

THE JUDGMENT OF THE GODS | 31

investigation of the Great King's death. What conclusion did you reach?"

"War intervened before I could proceed very far, and then Arda-Mulishi was deposed, so I stopped looking. It was the judgment of the gods."

"Who recommended you for this position?" Uncle asked.

"The Great King."

"But the Great King does not usually reach down into the ranks of his soldiers to find and reward one individual, does he? So, I was you again: who sponsored you, Captain?"

"I cannot say," Azizu finally said.

"Cannot, or will not."

"I cannot say."

"Then I guess we will have to continue asking our little questions, won't we?" Uncle said. "You are dismissed, Captain."

Banu did not appear at all that day, and I worried about what had happened to him. Truth be told, however, I did not know how to reach him, and was not sure that I wanted to.

We ate out that night, venturing down the winding back ways of Nineveh to one of the shops that lined Garden Street. They had a spiced fresh lamb fixed with herbs and late vegetables and olive oil that even at this cold time of the year was something well worth fighting for. The place was filled to the brim. The patrons were as raucous as black-headed crows jostling each other for scraps, the cymbals and drums kept warring with one another to beat a tune upon our deaf ears, and the girls, well, the girls were simply good enough to eat. We finally left the place satiated and satisfied, and just a little bit drunk.

Uncle belched. "That was, urrrp, that was splendiferous!"

But a few blocks away we lost track of where we were, and became uncertain of the neighborhood, which was far less fine than the one we had just been visiting. Suddenly I noticed a couple of toughs trailing a half street away, and I nudged Uncle in the ribs.

"Whaaat?" he burped again.

I nodded rearward, and slowly reached under my cloak to

draw my long, curved knife, hiding the glint. When the thugs rushed us, we were ready, and I carved my initials in one's belly while Uncle slit the throat of the other. A third man, hovering just beyond the rest, abruptly turned tail and ran off.

The villain whom I had sliced groaned in the mud and offal of the open sewer.

"Who sent you?" I asked.

When the man failed to reply, I shook him, like the rag doll he was.

"Who?" I repeated, pressing upon his wound.

"Ohhh," he groaned, "oh stop, please. I don't know. An officer. Paid me three Ishtars. Said two foreign folk would be at Kurbanu's. One with a scar on his right cheek"—I looked quickly at the slash on Uncle's face—"Ohhh."

We would get no more out of this one.

When we found our way home, I told Uncle what the man had said.

"Someone does not like us making inquiries," he said.

* * * * * * *

WONDER OF WONDERS, Prince Banu secured for us an interview with his grandmother on the next afternoon. We were escorted to the Royal Palace of Great King Sennacherib, where once again we were blindfolded, and led through a maze of rooms and passageways, until we were deposited on comfortable couches in a small waiting area. There we abided for some time until we heard the slight rattle of a bead screen being opened.

"My grandson says you wish to ask me about the Great King my husband's passing." The words were barely audible, but I detected the faintest trace of an accent, just as I could smell the barest essence of some exotic perfume. Perhaps it was myrrh or some other frankincense that I had never before encountered. Like this woman of power, it was rare and seductive and potent.

"What can you tell us of the officer known as Captain Azizu?" Uncle wanted to know.

THE JUDGMENT OF THE GODS | 33

"Tell you? I can tell you nothing," she said.

"But you recommended him for advancement five years past."

"That may be true," she said, "but I receive advice constantly from many different quarters, and I can scarcely remember every person whom I may have sponsored, particularly a man of low birth."

"I did not say he was of low birth."

"Perhaps I assumed it."

"You are not native to this region?"

"I was born in Calneh. My father was the Governor there, head of the family that once ruled the area. The Great King visited Calneh while he was yet in the House of Succession; he was captivated, and begged my father for the favor. So I became his Second Queen."

"Who was First Queen?"

Zakutu coughed before replying: "Tashmetum-Sharrat."

"She was Assyrian?"

"Yes."

"She was the mother of Crown Prince Ashur-Nadin-Shumi, he who was made King of Babylon by his father?"

"Yes."

"Ashur-Nadin-Shumi was betrayed to the Elamites twelve years ago?"

"Yes."

"No one knows who betrayed him?"

"Yes."

"The First Queen was also the mother of Arda-Mulishi and Nabu-Sharru-Usur?"

"Yes."

"These men are accused of murdering the Great King Sennacherib, their father?"

"Yes."

"But they did not kill their father?"

A long silence, and then: "This interview is over, impertinent little man."

* * * * * * *

ON THE SEVENTH day, we again met the Great King Esarhaddon at Fort Sargon, northeast of Nineveh. We went through the same routine as before.

"What have you Greeks learned?" the monarch asked. "Time presses. I must enter into my capital city tomorrow, the eighth day of Adaru, at the hour chosen by my priests, or face further unrest. You see, gentlemen, how I am become even more of a prisoner of my office than my two disgraced brethren."

The three of us sat there on a bench, Uncle Telemachos in the middle, Prince Banu to his right, and I to his left. Once again I acted as intermediary.

"We have examined the circumstances surrounding the passing of Great King Sennacherib," Uncle said. "We have interviewed the officer who was there, and we have investigated some of the events that occurred. The statue of the god Nisroch was undermined over a long period by the hand of the killer, who toppled the image onto the outstretched body of your father. This much is without question."

Then Telemachos said what he had to say to make his tale more palatable: "What I speak now is speculation, for I cannot prove any of it. The testimony indicates that the room was empty of priests, acolytes, or any visitors both before and after the Great King's murder. There is no entrance to the temple save the main door, and this was closely guarded by Captain Azizu and his thirty men. Although these soldiers are no longer available to be interviewed, we talked with one of their colleagues. What he told us largely confirms the officer's account."

"But if no one was there, my father must have been killed by the gods, as the priests have indicated," came that almost disembodied voice.

"Not so," Telemachos said. "He was murdered, and the murderer had long planned his passing, knowing of his nocturnal habits in visiting the god. The only man in the room, other than the Great King himself, was Captain Azizu. Therefore, only he

THE JUDGMENT OF THE GODS | 35

could have committed the sacrilege. Only he had the means and the opportunity."

"Azizu?" echoed both Esarhaddon and his son.

"But how? And why?" the Great King continued. "Everyone knows him to be a loyal and faithful servant to the state."

"Consider, Great King, that we only have his word as to the sequence of events. He ushered the guards out of the temple following their usual advance inspection of the premises, and escorted the Great King Sennacherib to his place before the statue of the god Nisroch. I believe that he then struck him senseless with the end of his spear; or perhaps he waited until the Great King was lying prone upon the floor, when he was most vulnerable, and violated him then. The body would have fallen without making any sound that could have been heard by the untrained troops roaming the perimeter outside. During part of this period he was unavailable to his troops, for when Sergeant Yari called to him for help, he did not immediately respond. This was unusual enough to be remembered later.

"Then the officer returned to his usual post for a time, making certain that his back was occasionally visible to his guards. When he reckoned that enough of an interval had passed, he crept forward, pushed over the previously loosened image onto the body of the Great King, obliterating at the same time the wound upon his master's head that he himself had rendered, and then yelled as the statue shattered itself upon the floor. When the soldiers rushed in, he was already bending over the deceased body of the Great King, trying to make the dead come alive, and there was nothing anyone else could do. The subsequent search of the building turned up no one, of course, because there was no one to be found. The guards naturally believed the death to be the act of the god whom Sennacherib had offended.

"As to the why of it, this is what we know, mighty King. The Prince Arda-Mulishi was briefly heir to the throne after the unfortunate death of his full brother, King Ashur-Nadin-Shumi, who was himself betrayed to the Elamites while he was serving as subsidiary King of Babylon for his father. But Arda-Mulishi was not the charming and intelligent man that his elder had been, and so he fell out of favor with the Great King. Despite the ministrations of the First Queen, you were named to his place in the House of Succession. All of this happened eleven years ago. Queen Tashmetum-Sharrat, where is she now?"

"She dwells in the palace of the late Great King Ashur-Nasir-Apli at the Holy City of Ashur," came the rough reply. "She and my mother did not get along."

"No, they did not get along," Uncle said, "and that was one of the problems. Second Queen Zakutu wanted to be First Queen, but she could not assume that role, because Tashmetum-Sharrat was Assyrian, and Zakutu, whose original name was Naqi'a, was Phoenician, or, if truth be told, Calnehan. Calneh, as I know very well, is a port town not very far south of the village Atalur, where we landed on our journey here. It is also the seat of governance for the entire region, is it not?"

"I believe this is so," the Great King said.

"Does the town of Qarqara fall within its control?"

"I believe this is so."

"Captain Azizu was a native of that place, and I think that he either knew or was connected to one of the Second Queen's relations, and that that cousin recommended him to her. She made him her man, and she sponsored him five years ago for the vacant Captaincy of the Royal Household Guards.

"Your father was troubled in his mind after the death of his eldest son, and the subsequent destruction of the city of Babylon. He believed that he had committed sacrilege, but was bound to the prophecy that he had himself commissioned from the priests, that Babylon could not be rebuilt again for a period of seventy years. Once written down, the dictum ensnared him, and there was nothing he could do. But he *could* change the succession back to the next eldest son, the full brother of his much beloved Ashur-Nadin-Shumi.

"I believe that Queen Zakutu learned of his intention, and I believe she took the action she considered appropriate to preserve your inheritance. This is one explanation. You may

THE JUDGMENT OF THE GODS | 37

accept or reject it, as you will."

I gasped out loud at his effrontery, and so, I think, did the prince and his father.

"You have another theory?" Esarhaddon growled. He was not a happy man.

"The Prince Arda-Mulishi plotted with his younger brother to secure the throne, knowing that his father would never give it to him, subverted Captain Azizu with promises of advancement beyond his station, and murdered the Great King Sennacherib on the twentieth day of Tebetu in the year of the eponym, Nabu-Sharru-Usur.

"That is all I have to say about the matter."

We waited then in silence for a very long time, not moving even the smallest bit, lest we be struck down by the wrath of the Great King.

"This is my pronouncement," the Great King Esarhaddon finally intoned. He clapped his hands, and when his servants entered the room, he ordered them to record his words. "We thank the Greek merchants who have visited the center of the earth, and who have rendered us a great service. As a token of our regard, we grant unto them special trading rights with the Kingdom of Assyria, all taxes to be remitted for the first five years of the agreement. Record it!" he demanded. "Further, the stranger named Te-le-ma-khu is to be given 100 gold pieces, and together with his party will depart our kingdom by the start of the New Year, bringing the good tidings of his new fortune to his homeland.

"However, the stranger who is named Akhu-Ilai will remain in Nineveh as chief of his station, and will be given a house of his own, with a *Turtanu* chosen by me to supervise that place, and servants and women to satisfy his every wish. He will have his own 100 lots of gold, and he will be recorded on the tablets as a man of position and power, as one who may advise the Great King on all matters relating to the west, and as friend and companion to the Great Prince in the House of Succession.

"Let this be recorded forever on the tablets of stone, let no man expunge my words or alter them in any way, lest they be condemned by the gods to unceasing torment.

"A copy of this document will be sent to you."

We heard him rise from his throne and begin to exit the room. Abruptly, he stopped and said: "Oh yes, I nearly forgot. Captain Azizu is hereby appointed as your new *Turtanu*, Akhu-Ilai."

* * * * * * *

LATER THAT EVENING, Uncle took me aside and looked me in the eye. "Be careful, nephew," he warned. "You know too much, and we have made great enemies these past few days."

"And great friends too," I said.

"And great friends too," he said, laughing and clapping me on the back.

Not long thereafter, Uncle and the rest of our party departed for home, carrying with them this account that I have made of the strange and curious adventures that we had faced together.

I shall miss him, grandsire, as I miss you now. But when you see your dear son again, when you meet Telemachos the son of Homeros, kiss him once in the exuberance of first greeting, and then let him kiss you once again on my behalf.

I do not know whether I shall see you again in this life, but so long as I have the power to ink a word upon a papyrus sheet or etch a line upon a tablet of clay, you will hear the echo of my voice within your soul, you will feel the wine-kissed wind of my breath touching your hoary brow, and you will laugh out loud once more for the pleasure of it.

This, I think, is the true judgment of the gods.

OCCAM'S RAZOR

"FIND US THE Templar treasure," said Pope John, tapping his cane on the floor to punctuate his speech, "Or you will experience first-hand the flames that consumed that devil-worshipper, Jacques de Molay."

* * * * * * *

OUR ADVENTURE HAD begun six months earlier in England. I have previously recorded several of the investigations of my illustrious master, the *Doctor Invincibilis* William of Occam, O.F.M., into matters insidious and criminous; but I could not relate until now his greatest feat of cogitation, for he charged me with the holiest of oaths never to speak of this affair again while he yet drew breath. The Red Death having claimed his dear life this past year, I am finally free to set down the story of the remarkable events which threatened our very lives and souls.

In November of the year 1323 my Master received a summons from the Holy Father, instructing Friar Occam to appear before a Tribunal at Avignon no later than the first day of May following. This was in response to a circular letter issued by Master William supporting the Declaration at Perugia of his friend Michael de Cesena, Father General of the Franciscan Order, that Jesus Christ and his apostles had owned nothing but the clothes on their backs, a position subsequently condemned by the Pope, who now threatened both Cesena and his followers with excommunication. Accordingly, my Master took formal leave from his teaching position at the University of Oxford, with every intention of returning there as soon as he had been cleansed of any theological taint.

We made a March crossing to Calais during a break in the weather, and for the first time I understood full well the torments awaiting evildoers in Hell. The town of Avignon is located in the southeastern corner of France, and given the foul condition of that country's roads, it took us almost six weeks to find our way south, making several stops along the way.

We entered Avignon near the end of April, and took lodging at Saint Anaclète, an establishment of our Order of Friars Minor in the southeast section of the town, just outside the walls. The town had been leased by Pope Clement V in 1309 as a fief from the King of Sicilia, but it always seemed to me a small and very crowded place, eminently suited to the poverty of mind exhibited by its rulers. Tucked into a bend of the Rhône River, the city had developed from an ancient settlement on the Rocher des Doms. This oblong hill was protected by a decaying Roman wall, and on it four great structures fought for space: the Citadel itself, overhanging the river; the official residence of the Bishops of Avignon, west of the Citadel; the Cathedral of Notre Dame des Doms, south of the Citadel and north of the Papal apartments; and the Palais des Papes, a large complex of buildings covering the south end of the crag. As the town had expanded, a second wall had been erected to protect the settlements south of the Rocher, but it too was soon eclipsed by new developments pushing beyond the limit of the battlements.

On our arrival Master William dispatched a note to His Holiness, informing him of our presence. For two weeks we received no response. Then—I remember the occasion well—a messenger dressed all in black banged on our door just after sunrise and handed my Master an official letter:

Feast of Saint Matthias the Apostle
Ad Gulielmum Occami, O.F.M.

Brother: thou shalt submit thyself to the authority of the Holy Father at the IIIRD hour of the morning II days hence.

†<u>Joannes XXII</u> *PM*

At the stated time we appeared before the Papal Palace, and were escorted to a private meeting room, not without some controversy, for I would have been excluded had not Master William insisted on my presence as a witness. An hour later the Holy Father shuffled into the room with the help of a cane. I had never seen his portrait, and was surprised to discover how frail he had become. At this time he had already reached his eightieth year, and was bent over with affliction. His white bushy eyebrows and cherubic face minded me of the elves my grandfather had described to me as a boy. The Pope took his seat on a dais to the right, and then stared at us for several minutes.

"So, even in this small matter you disobey us, Brother William," he finally said in a barely audible whisper.

"Forgive me, Holy Father," replied my Master, "But I have come to rely so heavily on Brother Thaddæus that I could not conceive the idea that he might be excluded."

"Then he may remain," the Pope said. "Father William, did you ever meet the heretic Jacques de Molay, last Master of the Order of the Knights of the Temple of Solomon?"

My Master started. "No, Your Grace. I was a young man when he was arrested, and still a student when he was executed in 1314."

"Yes," Joannes said, "But your Master at Oxford knew Molay, and through him you have been tainted."

Friar Occam hesitated a moment before answering. "What you say is true in the first part, Holy Father, but I never met the man, and I know very little about him except what idle gossip

THE JUDGMENT OF THE GODS | 43

has reported."

"The Templars are everywhere," said the Pope. "Their evil has never been extirpated, because the wicked idol they worshipped was never found by King Philip. Now they are circulating rumors that *we* were somehow involved in the deaths of their Grand Master a decade ago, and even of our predecessor and the King himself later that year. These are lies. Yet even lies can harm the innocent, and should these tales continue unabated, our Papacy itself could be at risk.

"We have heard of your investigation into the poisonings of the Oxford dons, and how you uncovered the foul murderer of young Vincent Garnier two years since, and we have equal need of your services. We therefore charge you to examine the deaths of Clemens V and Philip IV of beloved memory to determine whether their passings were unnatural, and if so, who killed them and why. We should not be displeased to hear that the Templars were involved. You are further ordered to recover the Templar treasure and to bring it to us privily." He drew a sheet from beneath his robe. "This warrant gives you the authority to question anyone in the realm, even King Charles, regarding these matters." He handed it to Brother William.

My Master considered his reply carefully. "These events, Holy Father, are perhaps best left to God's discretion. It has been a ten-year since the last Preceptors were executed or imprisoned, and longer than that since the Templars were suppressed. Scarce anyone who held a position of authority in the Order still lives. I have found through experience that the quicker such inquiries are made, the greater the probability of success. I do not believe that success is likely in this case."

Pope John sniffed. "We are not concerned with your reservations," he said. "If we are dissatisfied with the speed of your inquiries, we may undertake the suppression of a second order, the Friars Minor. Your Master Cesena has already defied our writ, and we have summoned him here to account for his actions. His fate, your fate, even your young companion's fate, are entirely in your hands. Do not disappoint us, Brother William.

The pyres can easily be relit. Now kiss our ring and be gone."

And thus we were dismissed.

* * * * * * *

LATER THAT EVENING we sat in our quarters, somberly sipping herbal tea and dining on hard bread and harder cheese. Master William had been uncommonly quiet much of the afternoon, and I had learned never to disturb his contemplations. "Well, young Thaddæus," he finally said, "What do you make of this day's events?"

"His Holiness is a hard taskmaster," I said.

"Indeed. But the challenge is still the most daunting we've faced since the Ebanus Equerry. Yes, we need a plan." He began pacing up and down the small room, his hands interlaced behind his back, his brows drawn tightly down over his eyes in concentration. "The lapse of time means that we can gain no first-hand impressions from anyone; even those who may have actually witnessed the events will have selectively edited them in their own minds during the ensuing years. Some may have even been ordered to do so.

"As always, we must ask ourselves these questions: if a crime took place, who had the opportunity to commit it? Who, having the opportunity, also had the will to effect it? Who, having the opportunity and will, had the means to carry it out? Who, having opportunity, will, and means, would have benefited from its possible commission? The answer to the latter question may be the only one we can truly satisfy at this late date. However, we must first determine the circumstances of each death, and who of those in attendance at each passing might still be living."

He turned to me. "As usual, Thaddæus, I will require you to record in detail everything that you see. Now, my boy, let us consider the final mystery placed before us. Please fetch me the speculum."

I carefully removed the instrument from the backpack where it had been specially cradled. It was a curved piece of metal, almost round in shape and highly polished to a supernally bright sheen. The alloy was quite unlike anything I have seen before or since, having a slight greenish tint that seemed to glow from within. On its back were inscribed a curious set of characters, like Roman letters in reverse, in a language I could not translate; my Master never told me where he had acquired the piece, although he did claim familiarity with the words.

Master William placed the mirror on his knees. As he made his preparations, he said: "What do you know about the Templars, Thaddæus?"

"Oh, sir, there are many stories about them, most of them bad. I do know the Order was suppressed by Pope Clement the year I was born. They are said to have practiced unholy rituals upon each other and the foulest kind of black magic, and to have worshipped an idol of Satan in the form of an obscene head."

"Don't believe everything you hear," said Friar Occam. "Every Order has its stray sheep, certainly. But I am utterly convinced that the Knights Templar were mostly righteous men who were unjustly accused of crimes that they never committed, and that their chief accuser, King Philip le Bel, profited greatly by their suppression. Now, let's see, where are we?"

He fiddled with the device on his lap, and suddenly it began to turn, slowly at first, then picking up speed. I could not see how it was being impelled, but Master William held his hands equidistant from the speculum as it rose slowly up from his legs. It began to whine as it glowed brighter and brighter, then turned on end so its top was facing outward towards me. "Don't be afraid, lad," my Master said. "Come closer and gaze into the mirror."

I crept nearer and looked in wonder upon the bright image of the thing. It seemed to me that a picture was forming on its upper surface, a vision of men dressed all in armor with piebald standards, crowded around a curious reliquary containing the faint outline of a face drawn on a white backdrop. There was no doubt in my mind that the picture was that of a bearded man, although the shading somehow seemed all wrong. The men appeared to be praying to the relic. Their expressions reflected joy and sanctity, not depraved debauchery, and they treated the object with great reverence. I could not tell where they were, except that the room was small and fully enclosed, lit only by flickering candlelight. I wanted to reach out and touch the image, but when I tried to do so, one of the knights turned and looked me straight in the eyes, as if he could actually see me, and I woke with a start from my trance.

"What did you experience, Thaddæus?" my Master asked.

After I had related my vision, Master William pondered these wonders for a few moments, before saying: "What you saw was the present, not the past. Those were Templars praying in their Temple, reduced though it might be in pomp and circumstance. If we can find that place, we will also discover their treasure, although I do not think the Holy Father will thank us for our efforts." He sighed. "Sufficient unto the day is the evil thereof. Off to bed with you, my son. We have much to do on the morrow."

* * * * * * *

THE NEXT MORNING, I awoke at sunrise to the droning of my Master's prayers, rousing myself reluctantly from my warm bed. After a brief repast, we hied ourselves to the Papal Apartments, where we began questioning the servants there, quickly determining those few who had been present under the previous administration. Chief among these was Frère Ambrosin, a man of some fifty years who now had achieved the position of Majordomo to the Papal household. A fringe of gray hair surrounded his pointed bald pate, making it look like nothing so much as a large, naked boulder poking up through dried, faded grass, the rock cracked and weather-stained by the elements.

"I'm a busy man," he said. "Whatever do you want?"

"Just a little of your time, Brother," my Master said. "And some of your memories. His Holiness has given me leave to question you on these matters. During the time of Papa Clemens,

God rest his memory, you were serving in the household here, were you not?"

"In truth, sir, I entered the late Pope's service in the year 1303, when he was still Archbishop of Bordeaux. Bertrand de Got, as he was known then, was a kind master to me, and I stayed with him when he was elevated to the papacy two years later." He scratched his bare head. "What's this about, sir? Have I done something wrong?"

Master William smiled. "No, nothing, Frère Ambrosin, please reassure yourself on that account. I just want to know something about the late Pope's health."

"His health, sir?" The majordomo looked puzzled. "Well, it was never very good, even from the beginning of his reign. He had the first of his 'spells,' as he used to call them, about a year after his election, following an argument with King Philip over those devil-worshippers the Templars, and was laid abed for a month and continued ill for more than four. Thereafter they'd come upon him at irregular times, often after some unpleasantness or another. Men in high stations seem to have an unending stream of such difficulties. Over the years these attacks steadily got worse, and finally he died of the last of them."

"Tell me more about these 'spells'," my Master said.

"Oh, they were terrible, sir," the monk said. "He'd have these pains in the belly something fierce, and would be doubled up and tossing about all night, often getting no rest at all, and he couldn't keep anything down, sometimes for days on end. Oh, we often prayed to God Almighty for his relief. I thought the first 'spell' would kill him for sure, it went on so long, but he finally recovered some of his health early in '07, though never like before. The attacks began again two years later, and with each he gradually weakened, until the final episodes caused him to shit blood and spit black bile sometimes. He suffered as much as any holy martyr, sir, I can tell you." He crossed himself.

"Who treated him when he had these attacks?" asked Master William.

"Well," said Ambrosin, "The Holy Father put great store in

the physicians, and one of them who provided him with some relief was eventually made Archbishop, I think, somewhere in the Germanies. So, there was always a well-trained doctor present, and I can tell you he received the best of care. In the end, even the King took an interest."

"Indeed?" my Master said.

"Oh yes. You see, the Holy Father left Avignon early in 1313 to visit his nephew at Carpentras, staying at Castle Monteux for over a year. But his health continued to decline, until finally King Philip became concerned and sent his own physician from Paris. The King himself visited the Pope before Christmas, making a hard winter's journey to comfort a sick friend." He looked around the room, and lowered his voice: "They had a terrible row, you know."

"Really?"

Ambrosin nodded his head. "The King wanted Papa Clemens to sign some document or other regarding those Templar people, which he finally did, because I had to witness it, and King Philip thought I couldn't read." He chuckled to himself. "Those great men never thought very much of me, just because I was born a peasant. They would talk around me like I wasn't even in the room. All except the Holy Father.

"But the Pope continued to worsen, and the following Spring he decided to go home to his family in Gascony. Just after starting out from Carpentras he received a letter that upset him greatly, and he took to his bed that evening, never to rise again. They were able to carry him to Roquemaure-on-the-Rhône before he expired. Oh, sir, I tell you he died in God's good grace."

My Master was appropriately somber. "Brother Ambrosin, was there anything about his final illness that seemed at all unusual?"

The Majordomo said: "Now that you mention it, sir, I tended the Holy Father during his last days, and I did notice his fingertips becoming somewhat discolored. I didn't think much of it at the time, because he was so clearly failing. Also, I combed his hair daily, and it began to come out in clumps during that final week. But he had a fever, and sometimes sick people do lose all their hair. So, I don't know anymore."

"You mentioned a letter that Papa Clemens received near the end."

"Yes, sir," said the monk, "But it was never found after he died, and I have no knowledge of who sent it or what it contained."

"Thank you, Brother Ambrosin," Master William said. "You have been most kind."

We next interviewed the Chief Cook, one Master Manosque, a rather thin fellow who looked as if he'd never eaten a good meal in his life. His whole face was a frown.

Again Brother William introduced himself and asked Manosque about his service.

"I cook for Clemen-Pope six years," he said. "I cook good."

"I am quite certain that no one would criticize your cuisine," said my Master, "But I would like to know about the Holy Father's stomach problems."

"Bad, very bad," Manosque said. "Tummy make noise all time. Pains, gas, loose turds. All bad. Sometime no can eat. Not my food. My food good. My food fresh." He waved his arms around like a windmill, obviously much agitated.

Master William stifled a smile. "I have heard nothing but praise about your fine dinners. Now tell me, who prepared the Pope's meals when he left Avignon?"

"Pope leave 'Vignon?" asked the cook.

"Yes, you remember, the year before he died, Papa Clemens went to his nephew's castle."

"I fix. I fix all Clemen-Pope's food. No one else fix," Manosque said.

"And was he well there?" asked Master William.

"No, no, very bad at Montus. Eat little, burp much. I fix good food, but...." The chef's shoulders lifted in resignation.

"What about when the Holy Father left Carpentras to go to Gascony?" my Master inquired.

"I follow. Pope eat bad. I bring good food, but he all white.

50 | ROBERT REGINALD

He have paper in hand. Hand shake. He fall on floor. He cry for God. God come." He crossed himself, and we followed suit. "Very sad. He good master. New master mean. Very sad."

And that was all we were able to get out of the eloquent Master Manosque. We talked with several other members of the Pope's staff, but they could add little, until we reached Brother Daniel Jacquelot, a man in his forties shaped like a pear, with bulging stomach and normal-sized chest and arms.

"Brother Daniel," my Master said, "Can you tell us anything about Papa Clemens's passing?"

Jacquelot had a way of answering every query with another question. "Well, he'd been ill for some time, hadn't he? I didn't have daily contact with him, no one did, despite what they might say. When he was sick, which was often, he eschewed the company of everyone except a few relatives and confidantes, and he had promoted so many of the former into the latter that there were always several cousins and nephews about.

"I think what brought the crisis on was the business over the Templars. The Pope was a good man, don't misunderstand me, but he wanted to be loved, and King Philip le Bel utterly dominated him. In the last year of his life he became increasingly unhappy about what he had been forced to do with these knights. He never believed the stories about their supposed misdeeds. On several occasions he told me that he just hoped Molay and his cronies would die peacefully in prison and solve his problem. After all, they were all old men, as old as the Pontiff.

"But they didn't die, and finally the King came to him at Carpentras and demanded that Molay and Charnay be publicly tried. You see, under the law, Philip had to have the Order suppressed and its leaders condemned by the Pope for the Templar property which the King had already confiscated to remain legally in his hands, supposedly for a new crusade, a crusade that never materialized.

"Then the King's man, that snake Nogaret, came to him after we had left Carpentras for Gascony, and gave him a message, perhaps from his master. The Pope yelled something at him, then collapsed and never recovered."

Master William paused for a moment before replying. "Did the Holy Father experience any unusual symptoms during his final days?"

"Who could say for sure?" Daniel said. "I only saw him once or twice that week, and he looked pale and very ill. I do remember that when we prepared his body for transport a few days later, it seemed to me somewhat discolored, at least compared to others I had seen, and this quite shortly after death; but each corpse tells its own story, doesn't it?"

Brother Daniel had nothing further to add, and we could find no other servants or staff to provide us with new details about the long-ago passing of Clemens V. Later that evening, my Master asked me about the day's proceedings.

"Well, sir," I said, "It's obvious to me that the Pope had been sick for many years, and that he probably died of his ailment, whatever other factors may have contributed to his death."

"Perhaps," was all Master William would say. "But still I find it curious that his persistent illness seemed to produce such contrary symptoms near the end."

* * * * * * *

WE SPENT A DAY settling our accounts in Avignon, then journeyed north to Paris to interview the King and his ministers concerning the death of King Philip IV and the Templar treasure. When we arrived, we took quarters at the Franciscan Monastery of Saint Tiron, and sent a note to the Palace requesting an audience, which we received three days later. Charles IV, called le Bel after his father, was then about thirty years of age, and like all of his family, strikingly well formed. He had succeeded his brother, King Philip le Long, in 1322, and was now calling himself Holy Roman Emperor, following the deposition of Emperor Ludwig by Pope John just two months earlier. Common gossip held that great sums had changed hands for this little favor.

We were led to a private antechamber, where we made our

obeisances, and my Master gave our warrant to His Majesty, who passed it to his minister for consideration. They conferred for several minutes before returning the document. "What do you seek, Brother William?" the King asked.

"Only the truth, Sire," my Master said. "His Holiness wishes to know the circumstances of your father's passing ten years ago."

"Does he indeed. There are many truths, Frère Guillaume, some of them truer than others. Our late father died cursed by that devil-worshipper Molay, and he suffered greatly for his sins. But did you know that he also died cursed by his three sons? Ah, now that surprises you.

"Early in the year 1314 Philip the un-Fair arrested our wife and the wives of our two royal brothers, accused them of adultery on the false witness of our sister, Isabella of England, and then had them imprisoned. Our lovely Blanche was scarcely eighteen years of age. She was pure and innocent and guileless, and there was nothing we could do to save her. She was taken away to a nunnery at Maubuisson, and we had to divorce her. So, do not ask us of our father. He died unlamented by his family."

Master William considered his next words carefully. "But what were the specific circumstances of King Philip's passing?"

"You vex us, Frère Guillaume, you do not listen to what we say," the King said. "Yet, out of respect for the Holy Father who has given us so much, we will answer. *Nota bene*: the King our father had gone to hunt at Pont Saint Maxence in early November, and he took ill in the woods there on the fourth day of that month. We saw him stop suddenly beneath a tree, turn white, stiffen, clutch his head, and slump over his saddle. There was no doctor present, but his aide, Master Rodolphe, went to him immediately, and said he had no pulse. However, he soon recovered his wits, and was taken by boat to Poissy, thence by horse to Essonnes, and then by litter to Fontainebleau. By this time he had suffered a second attack, worse than the first, and he finally succumbed there on the twenty-ninth."

THE JUDGMENT OF THE GODS | 53

"Who visited him *in extremis*?" my Master asked.

"Those of the lords temporal and lords spiritual who arrived in time came to his bed to receive his blessing," King Charles said. "They included the Archbishop of Bourges, the Cardinal Bishop of Avignon and Porto, the Abbot of Cluny, the Count of Poitiers, the Archbishop of Embrun, the Viscount of Lomagne, the Cardinal de Got, and a few others of lesser rank. He then called our brother, Louis X of blessed memory, to his side, and told him: 'Ponder these words, young Louis: "What is it to be King of France?"' Much of what he said during that last week made no sense. A few days later he perished, and his body was returned to Paris."

"Your Majesty mentioned Lomagne and Got. Were they not related to the late Papa Clemens?" asked Master William.

"They were. Lomagne was his nephew, we believe. As you may have already heard, the Pope had a certain affinity for his own family," the King said with the flash of a smile that quickly vanished. "Now, we have other duties to which we must attend. There is nothing further we can tell you about this matter. We wish you *bon voyage*, Frère Guillaume." And he waved us away.

Later that afternoon we questioned the Court Physician, Odonar d'Artevelde, who had served the Kings of France for a quarter century. The Doctor was a pompous little toad of about sixty years, with a long gray beard, balding pate, and flamboyant robes. I would have thought him a magician or wandering actor had I not known otherwise.

"You were not present when the King suffered his first attack?" my Master asked.

"Indeed, I was not!" Odonar said. "The King was on holiday, and I was in Paris. Of course, when I heard that His Majesty had fallen ill, I left immediately, and reached Fontainebleau on the same day that the King's litter arrived."

"And what was the King's condition when you first examined him?" Master William asked.

"His humors were clearly out of balance, particularly the *choler*, giving his skin a yellowish cast; and as a result he had suffered a slight paralysis in his left side, making it difficult for him to sit long in the saddle, although he could speak and reason without impairment. I was told that the first attack had affected his heart, and this I could confirm with my trained eye, that there was still a weakness of limb and shortness of breath common to those afflicted by such ailments.

"Yet, even with all of these difficulties, he seemed in very good spirits and on his way to a good recovery. Overall, his body was still strong and virile, and I felt that he had an excellent chance of living at least another five or ten years, if he could avoid excessive strain and excitement; and I did not hesitate to tell him so. However, being the prudent man that he was, he updated his will and made his confession to the Cardinal."

"The Cardinal?" Friar Occam said. "Oh, do you mean Got?"

"No, no, the other one, you know, Duèse. He and the King were old friends, and he had hurried up from Avignon when he heard about le Bel's misfortune. Ha, he must have ridden a few horses to death to get there as quickly as he did, and he a man of seventy." He chortled to himself, then sobered very quickly. "It was a funny thing, though. After that, the King just seemed to lose heart. Within two days it was obvious he was dying, and he called his children around him to give them his final blessing. I did everything I could. But he broke into a rash and the phlegmatic humor overwhelmed the others, filling his lungs with fluid. I've never seen anything quite like it. He should have lived." The physician's shoulders slumped.

"And then his sons followed him to the grave one by one, all young men, too, first bold Louis and then Philip the Tall, with little Jean squeezed in between, just five days old at his death. The family is cursed, no doubt about it. It was those thrice-damned Templars. Molay jinxed the King and his sons as the flames claimed him. I was there, and I still have nightmares about it. I remember Molay politely inviting the Pope and King to join him before God's throne by year's end, and then the Preceptor Geoffroi de Charnay shouting out: 'The shroud shall claim you, my Lords, you cannot escape the shroud.' It was chilling, I tell you." He shuddered.

Master William thanked him graciously for his time, and we retired to our cells at the abbey for the evening.

"Master," I said, after we had eaten our simple meal, "I don't understand. Both of these men appeared to have died natural deaths, and yet the Holy Father seems much concerned about the circumstances." This, one must remember, was decades before the terrible scourge of the plague had made death a commonplace visitor to our households. "I also don't see how we will ever find these Templars, if indeed there are any members of that Order still living."

My kind and wise teacher just smiled, startled from his musings, and said: "As the Lord said to Job: 'Who is this that darkeneth counsel by words without knowledge?' Never fear, dear Thaddæus. All things come to those who wait."

* * * * * * *

SOMETIME IN THE MIDDLE of the night I came suddenly awake, shivering for lack of a cover, and abruptly realized that I was lying on a rough animal skin spread carelessly on the cold stone floor of a strange room, a place that I had no recollection of reaching. My Master lay supine beside me, snoring gently. The last thing I remembered from the previous evening was drinking a cup of wine freshly spilled out from a newly-tapped skin, and then toddling off to bed. Now my head ached abominably, as if Satan himself were stabbing it with a large pin, and I found it hard to gain my bearings. Nearby, a solitary candle barely illumined the area where we had been placed.

"Master," I said, "Master, wake up."

Friar Occam groaned and tried to sit up. "Where are we?" he asked. "What is this place?"

A voice behind us replied, "Welcome to the Paris Commanderie of the Military Order of the Knights of the Temple of Solomon. I regret that our accommodations are not what they were, but we were never slaves to comfort. I regret also the deception used in bringing you here, but no one must ever know of this place. However, we did obtain a set of your robes for your comfort."

While we quietly dressed, several of the brethren beyond the sphere of light began lighting the torches placed around the walls of the room, and I gasped when I realized that it was the same place that I had seen several weeks earlier in my vision. Gradually the figures became distinguishable, and I realized that they wore the same piebald standards as before. Their faces were covered with plain black masks.

"Brother William, I believe you have some questions to ask us," said their leader.

"Who are you?" my Master asked.

"You will excuse me, sir, if I limit myself to saying that I am the Grand Master of the reconstituted Order, duly elected by its surviving membership."

"The Templars were officially suppressed by Pope Clemens twelve years ago. By what right do you claim that usage?"

"By the rule established by the Council of Troyes, and by the traditions established by Hugues de Payens and the Nine Founders. Although we respect the Holy Fathers, past and present, they are only men, subject to the fallibility of the flesh or even, on occasion, to the wiles of the Devil. The evil that was done to us seventeen years ago was not the work of God, but the actions of two such men, one a King eager to fill his coffers, the other a Pope eager to curry favor with the King. God could not have sanctioned actions so abhorrent to everything taught us by our Lord Jesus Christ.

"This being the case, the Holy Father was in error, and his suppression of our Order, while legal under the canons of the Church, was contrary to God's will. Therefore, those of us who survived the King's depredations have continued the traditions of our brothers, and have re-established the Order as a secret society devoted to maintaining our special knowledge for the benefit of mankind. In this we have the blessing of Almighty God and his son Jesus Christ. We shall not again be destroyed."

THE JUDGMENT OF THE GODS | 57

Master William rubbed his eyes in weariness. "What of the charges levied against you?" he asked.

"Lies and fabrications," said the knight. "Oh, we do not claim perfection, sir. We are sinners all, imperfect vessels at best to be filled with God's grace. But we are innocent of the accusations made against us, as proven by the actions of our Grand Master, Jacques de Molay, who died the martyr's death with his Preceptor, Geoffroi de Charnay. God has punished the instigators of these crimes, and he will continue to punish them unto the thirteenth generation. Yea, I tell you that this Kingdom shall soon pay a fearful price for the iniquities of its kings, and like the ancient land of Egypt under the Pharaohs, it shall suffer a hundred years of plagues and wars and famines.

"As for the so-called Supreme Pontiffs, your young companion shall live to see two men calling themselves Pope, each supported by half the civilized world, one residing in Avignon, one in Rome. That schism shall forever destroy the power of the Popes."

"And what of the idol, the head men claim you worship?" my Master asked.

"Now, that is the greatest lie of all," said the Grand Master. "And yet there is a certain basis to the tale, for the Devil often mixes truth with falsehood to seduce the unwary. In the time of Christ the King of Edessa was a leper, and sent a letter to Jesus pleading for relief from his illness. But the Son of God had already been crucified by the Jews and Romans, and so one of his lesser disciples, Addai, was sent to Syria to convert that land. He brought with him a cloth that had covered the blessed body of Jesus in his tomb, and with it he cured King Abgar of his affliction. The monarch and his land embraced Christianity. The shroud remained in Syria for nine hundred years, until Samosata was occupied by the Saracens. They reluctantly traded the cloth to the Byzantine Emperor for several hundred Muslim prisoners, and the artifact was brought to Constantinople in 944, where it was most joyously displayed in Santa Sophia. The Mandylion, for such was its name, remained there until the city was sacked by the crusaders in the year 1204, at which time it was acquired by the Order of the Temple. When Acre fell in 1291, our treasures were moved to Cyprus, and thence to France.

"Everything that I have told you here is true. Yet these are just words. I could be lying, I could be deceived, I could be wrong. So let me show you the proof of what I say."

I saw him signal slightly with his left hand, and the ranks of the brethren abruptly parted. There I saw the face of my vision, the haunted visage of a thin, bearded man, his forehead crowned with thorns. The shroud was housed in a box that displayed the head only, the rest being folded underneath. I was overwhelmed with emotion, for there was no doubt in my mind that this cloth had once covered the blessed face of our Savior. I fell to my knees in reverence, my Master and the knights around us following suit.

"We have been told that the cloth must now leave us for a brief time," the Templar said, "and that young Thaddæus here shall serve as the instrument of God's will, since he is innocent in both body and soul. Therefore, see now the miracle of the shroud!"

He reached into the box, unfastened the cloth, and slowly, very gently drew forth the entire length of the burial covering, and I gasped again, for the image of Christ's body and the punishments it had suffered at the hands of the ignorant heathen were plainly evident for all to see, albeit shaded and delineated as if reversed in image. Here and there the fabric was spotted with Jesus's holy blood.

My Master crossed himself and exclaimed, "Glory be to God that I have lived long enough to see such a wonder firsthand! But you say we are to take this great gift away with us. Why? The Pope will only confiscate it if we bring it to him."

The Grand Master of the Templars said: "All I can tell you is that you will have need of it soon enough. As for the cloth, well, God protects his own, as he has protected this free Temple from discovery by the King. The shroud will eventually be returned to us unharmed. We have seen this in the visions God has been gracious enough to grant to us, and we also know that you, Gullielmus Magus, are his agent for good in the world, now and in the years to come. Let Brother Thaddæus be the carrier, and mark well my words: do not touch the shroud yourself, do not let any other person handle it except your young ward. *He* is the chosen." Then he stretched out his arms and embraced Master William, kissing him on each cheek: "Peace be unto thee, Brother, and good journey to you both."

* * * * * * *

THE NEXT MORNING we left Paris—for that is where we were, wonder to say—for Avignon, reaching the town in early June. The days were warm and fair on our journey, and I felt as happy then as I ever have, content with my life and what it had to offer. Every step of the way south I could feel the shroud burning on my back, folded there into its leather carrying case, but it was a pleasant warmth, reinforced by the sun's rays, and making me feel for the first time that I had much to contribute to the world. All roads were open to me. As we drew ever nearer to that old man tap-tapping his way around and 'round his gilded prison, I realized for the first time how sad a little life he must live, how constrained he must feel, and how joyless was his existence. I determined then and there to do something worthwhile with my life, and vowed to God that I would become a Templar if that were possible.

Pope John must have had spies watching for us, for no sooner had we returned to our cells at Saint Anaclète's when we received a message summoning us to audience the first thing the next morning. This time we were led to the ornate reception room of the Palais des Papes, where the Supreme Pontiff perched high on his great throne, surrounded by his cardinals and councilors. We entered and paid due homage to the leader of Western Christianity.

"Have you fulfilled your quest?" asked the Pope.

"We have, Your Grace," my Master said.

John waved his hands at the others in the room: "You may leave us." When they were gone, he said: "Make your report, then."

Friar Occam formally bowed, clasped his two hands together as if praying, and began: "You set us three tasks, Holiness. As to the first, we have investigated the death of your predecessor, Clemens V of blessed memory, and have made certain determinations." He then explained whom we had questioned and why, giving detailed summaries of their answers.

"Was he murdered?" the Pontiff asked.

"Possibly. His illness did change somewhat in his last days, following his meeting with Nogaret." Master William paused, as if considering his words more profoundly, and then I heard him expound for the first time that statement for which he later became most famous. "Yet I think not, for what can be done with fewer assumptions is done in vain with more. My own judgment is that Papa Clemens died a natural death, albeit one made more severe with anxiety. For the King had no need to dispose of him, since he already was the most pliant creature in all of France."

"Be careful what you say, Brother William," said the Pope, "Be very careful. And what of the King's death?"

"Ah, yes, Philip le Bel. Now, *that* is a problem of an entirely different order. The King suffered an attack of paralysis early in November, and despite a slight recurrence a week later, appeared to be recovering his health, with perhaps some slight weakness remaining in his side. Then his symptoms changed completely, following the visit of one of his friends, and he died very quickly thereafter. The simplest explanation for this is that the King was poisoned."

"And who killed him?" Pope John asked.

"Why, *you* did, Cardinal Duèse," my Master said.

The Holy Father started, and I expected him immediately to call in the guards and have us both arrested and executed on the spot. But he did no such thing, much to my surprise. Instead,

THE JUDGMENT OF THE GODS | 61

after a moment's silence, he asked: "Why would *I* do that?" He used the personal pronoun for the first time.

"Because you wished to be Pope, and you knew that the King had withdrawn his support of your candidacy, since he could not control you. The College of Cardinals was deadlocked, and the King was about to insist that his own man be elected. Without Philip, you could keep the balloting going indefinitely, until a compromise could be reached. It took you two years, but you finally achieved your goal."

"You have no proof of these...speculations?" Pope John asked.

"No, none."

"Then you will keep them to yourself on pain of death, and we shall make certain that you have no chance to recite them in a court of law. Now, what of the Templar treasure?"

My Master smiled a strange smile, turned up at one corner of his mouth. "Oh, we found it, Your Grace."

"What?" Clearly the Holy Father was not expecting this answer. "Where is it? I see nothing."

"You must open your eyes to see, Pontifex Maximus." He turned to me: "Thaddæus!" he commanded.

Then I retrieved the pouch from my back and carefully pulled the cloth forth where the Pope could not see. As I turned around I allowed the entire length of the shroud to unravel, holding it up as high as I could reach. And it seemed to me that the figure etched on the linen writhed and moved, and a deep voice spoke forth quite clearly, filling the room with its presence: "John, John, why persecutest thou me?"

The Pope screamed then, quite loudly for one so old, as if he had looked into the depths of Hell itself and seen his own place well prepared, and he yelled again, almost incoherently, "Take it away, take it away," spittle dribbling down his chin, his right hand waving futilely in the air. At a nod from my Master, I carefully folded the shroud and reverently put it away into its leather case. Guards and officials had already begun to respond to his shouts, and they seized us immediately.

After he had regained his composure, John ordered us

62 | ROBERT REGINALD

released and again cleared the room, save for a secretary. He looked down upon us sternly before pronouncing judgment: "Brother William, you will forget everything that has happened here, and you will swear never to reveal what you have learned to another soul, on the pain of instant excommunication and death by fire for you and your assistant."

My Master had no choice but to give his oath to that effect.

"You may go for now," said John, "But you will both remain within the boundaries of Avignon until I release you."

And once again we were dismissed.

* * * * * * *

LATER THAT DAY we were walking in the garden of the abbey, and I asked Master William: "Sir, I don't understand. Why did the Pope release us?"

He replied with a quote from Scripture: "'Many prophets and kings have desired to see those things which you see, and have not seen them; and to hear those things which you hear, and have not heard them.' The Holy Father knew that he could not cross a certain boundary, that the shroud would protect its own. That does not remove the danger entirely, my son, for Popes and Potentates have very short memories, and while we are within John's easy reach, we shall have to walk the walk of righteous men. Now, it is time for prayers, and I suggest to you that both we and he have urgent need of them."

He smiled broadly at my consternation and tossed my hair. "Never fear, young Thaddæus, the truth shall not easily be suppressed, and there shall come a day when the Templars and their shroud can once again be seen openly in the world."

* * * * * * *

NOW, THESE EVENTS took place a quarter century ago, in the Year of Our Lord 1324, when my wise and good Master, William of Occam, was just beginning to formulate his philosophies, and when we had many great adventures yet to come. I look back upon those days with wonder and with gratitude, and thank God Almighty that I had the chance to walk with giants upon the earth. And when I gaze into the speculum which Master William left me, I can see the cross on my surcoat reflected back at me, and remember his dear face which I miss so much. Amen.

OCCAM'S TREASURE

THEY CAME FOR US at the hour of the wolf, that time in the darkest part of the night when the Shrouded One stretches forth his shriveled hand and snatches up the souls of those wavering at the boundary 'twixt life and death, while their bodies are yet quivering with their last gasp of air.

The papal soldiers burst their way into the Monastery of Saint Anaclète in Avignon, not even attempting to secure the permission of Father Superior Pontien, rousting us from our cells, no more than half awake. They dragged us into the warm night air, and escorted us forthwith to the Palais des Papes, a large complex of buildings covering the south end of that crag which is called the Rocher des Doms, high above the city.

His Holiness, Papa John XXII, who scarcely deserved such an appellation, was waiting for us on his golden throne.

"So, Friar William, we find your overall demeanor as obstinate as it ever was," the old man whined.

In the year since our last meeting, the pope had developed a slight tremor in his left hand, or so it seemed to me.

"And you, Brother Thaddæus," he said, turning in my direction, "do you still have in your possession that ugly sackcloth you showed me last year?"

He was referring, of course, to the Holy Burial Shroud of our Lord and Savior, Jesus Christ.

"I do, Holiness," I said.

"Hmm," the pontiff said.

Then he said nothing for many minutes, leaving us standing

there before him, his eyes glazing over in reflection or fatigue or something else entirely. Not much more than a twelvemonth ago, in the year of Our Lord 1324, we had played a game of cat and mouse with the pope over the Templar treasure, and had come away from the confrontation with at least a stalemate. The much-touted wealth of that militant order of religious knights had turned out to be Our Lord's Shroud, over which we had been granted temporary custodianship by the new Grand Master of the Templars. Ever since then, we had been confined under house arrest in the papal town of Avignon, forbidden to venture outside the small city-state on the pain of instant excommunication and death.

"We have need of you again," he finally said, in a voice that was barely audible. "Our nephew, Boson Comte de la Bâteau, has been foully murdered this past fortnight."

"This is tragic news, Excellency," my dear master said, "but what has it to do with us? I would be happy to say a mass for the repose of his soul, but I see nothing else we can do."

The pontiff motioned to an aide, who stepped forward and put something in Father William's hand.

"These were found on the body of the deceased," the pope said, "or rather, within the corpus itself, resting on his tongue."

I watched as my master unwrapped an old coin from a piece of papyrus. A large numeral "IV" was inked on the scrap of paper. I didn't recognize the ruler on the disk.

"Was this the first such incident, Holiness?" Fra William asked.

Again we waited while the Holy Father framed his next response.

"No," he finally said. "There have been three previous killings, all of them involving individuals directly connected to us."

"What else has happened?" my teacher asked. "You've received something further, haven't you?"

The old man shifted on his throne and sighed, then nodded to his associate, Father Johad, who passed another document to Father William. My master took a moment to review the letter, and showed it to me. It read:

"To Ioannes XXII, who calls himself Pope:

"Jacques de Molay, Master of the Order of the Knights of the Temple of Solomon, reaches out from his grave to accuse you, Jacques Duèse, of heresy, murder, bribery, simony, and other crimes and misdemeanors unbecoming a prince of the Church, in that you schemed and manipulated and purchased your way onto the chair of Saint Peter. For these actions, he condemns you in the name of Jesus Christ to eternal damnation, unless you renounce your titles, offices, and emoluments, and become as a little child, without possessions, sees, or purse.

"He gives you until Michaelmas of this year to abdicate your throne and acknowledge the poverty of Jesus Christ and his followers. For every week that you delay, one of those connected to you shall render the ultimate penalty for your obstinacy. Should you fail to renounce the papacy by the date indicated, the power to do so shall be wrenched from your filth-covered hands.

"Maître Jacques de Molay
Les Chevaliers Nouveaux du Temple"

John coughed very loudly and cleared his throat.

"If we yield to such persuasion," he said, "we establish a precedent that others may employ against our successors; should we not abdicate within the next four months, many more of our dearly-beloved associates may meet a fate wholly undeserved by them; in either case we shall be made the harlequin of the Christian world, fit for nothing but mockery by those we attempt to guide, for we have no doubt that these rogues will very shortly make public their actions against us. Our rule

THE JUDGMENT OF THE GODS | 67

shall fail, and the thrice-damned Templars shall once again be re-established in their seats of power."

"We are Franciscans, not men of action," Fra William said. "The temporal authorities are certainly capable of dealing with such matters far better than we."

"So one might presume." The pope sighed. "But the matter has proved more troublesome than we expected. We have dispatched several individuals and squads of papal guards to investigate these crimes, Father Occam. The bodies of one such group were discovered several weeks ago in the Tournal District, blasted by some foul magic of Satan himself. So what are we to do?"

Then he began crying most piteously, a high thin sound, like that of a young girl who has just been thwarted in love.

My master waited until the pontiff had regained some control over himself, before saying: "You have three options, Holiness. You can acquiesce to the demands of these renegades. You can take no action, and let God sort out the consequences. You can fight back. You must realize, however, that should you opt for the latter course, whoever is behind this storm of terror may well escalate the price that you ultimately pay for the resolution of this mystery."

"We understand this perfectly well, Father William," the pope said. "Do not treat us like some six-year-old waif. We want *you* to find these resurgent Templars. Identify those responsible for these crimes, and we will take care of the rest. We shall give you letters granting you and your companion access into any house in France. Father Arlan d'Esprit, our trusted associate, shall be our eyes and ears in this matter."

I could tell from his manner that Father Occam was not much pleased with these proceedings, but truth to tell, he had very little choice in the matter.

"I shall need access to all of the reports collected on the previous deaths," my master said.

"Father Johad will provide these to you, as well as the coins and notes found on the others," came the reply.

"What about the bodies of the victims?" Father William asked.

"They were consigned unto the earth," the pontiff said.

"Can they be exhumed?"

The pope put his hand up to his mouth and chewed on the mottled web of skin between the thumb and forefinger.

"Is this truly necessary?" John asked.

"Do you wish this mystery to be solved?" my teacher said.

The primate sighed a second time.

"Very well," he said, turning to his aide. "Père Johad, draw up the appropriate order."

"Yes, Holiness," the priest said, bowing low.

Then we were released to return to our lodgings.

It was now the hour of the dove.

* * * * * * *

My ILLUSTRIOUS MASTER, the *Doctor Invincibilis* Father William of Occam, of the Order of Friars Minor, was primarily known at this time not for the rich philosophical tomes which he was to pen during his long exile in Germania, but as an *investigator veritatis*, or seeker after truth. Beginning with the terrible murders at Exeter College, in which Father Occam proved that the treacherous Master Morbinus had very slyly poisoned three of his fellow *magistri* in order to better his own position, my teacher's fame had spread rapidly through certain circles in England; and during the ensuing years, before he was abruptly summoned to the chair of Saint Peter, he was often called upon to resolve questions of life and death.

It was during these years that I first heard him develop that logical principle which became known even during his own lifetime as "Occam's Razor," which holds that "what can be done with fewer assumptions is done in vain with more."

As we broke our fast back at the abbey, I asked him about our meeting with the pope.

"I think, young Thaddæus," he said, "that our Holy Father

did not really want to give us this task, but felt that he had no choice in the matter. Things have advanced too rapidly, and his position is now seriously threatened."

"But who would attack the Holy Church?" I asked.

"Papa John has made many personal enemies who would delight in his fall from grace, including the Emperor Ludwig and our own Father Superior."

Then he took the coin that had been removed from Count Boson's mouth, and held it up to the light, turning it over once or twice.

"Most curious," he said, placing it on the bench in front of us.

I had never seen anything quite like it. The bright silver disk was a little larger than my thumb. On the obverse, it featured the bust of a clean-shaven man of perhaps thirty-five, his curly hair bisected over the crown of his head by a narrow band of cloth, the two ties of which draped down the nape of his neck. The portrait was framed by a fillet border.

The reverse of the coin bore the image of a seated, bearded man holding the small figure of a standing woman (appearing almost like an angel) in his right hand, and a floor-length staff in his left. She was offering him something. The *tableau* was framed on either side by two lines of large type, written in a language that I did not understand, whose letters consisted of a series of interconnected dots.

"What do you think?" my master asked.

"Well," I said, "the king on the front, if that's what he is, has a large, hooked nose and a protruding chin."

Father William smiled slightly and shook his head.

I tried again. "Although the coin looks newly minted," I said, "the style is not modern, and I suspect it may be much older than it appears."

"Very good," my teacher said, "what else?"

"The inscription uses non-Roman characters," I said. "If we knew the language in which it was written, we might be able to identify the time and place more accurately."

"Excellent!" he stated. "Why do you think this determination is important?"

"If the other three coins are similar to this," I said, "then the killer might be sending some hidden message by placing these artifacts in the victims' mouths."

"Yes," Occam said. "How shall we determine whence these derive?"

"I...." I paused for a moment. "I don't know, master."

* * * * * * *

THAT AFTERNOON WE again made our way to the Rocher des Doms to meet with Fathers Johad and Arlan d'Esprit. The former was a clean-shaven man of about fifty, clad in the rusty red robes of the Order of Saint Blaise, while his companion was perhaps twenty years his junior, tall and straight and bearded—and a fellow Franciscan!

Laid out on a small table before them were the implements from the earlier murders: three coins, three scraps of papyrus marked with Roman numerals, two of them badly discolored, and a bronze stiletto. It was immediately apparent that all four deaths were connected.

"These tokens and papers," my master asked, "all were found in the victims' mouths?"

"Yes," Johad said.

"Tell me about them."

"The first death occurred a month ago," Johad said. "Bishop Thoune, in town to visit the pope, was dining in the refectory of Saint Jude's, when he began gagging and collapsed onto the floor. They thought he had choked on something, but when they pried opened his jaws, all they found were these...things.

"The second victim was Sieur Phocion Duèse de La Pacaudière. He had come to Avignon to pay his respects to his papal cousin, but was stabbed to death one night while frequenting a certain establishment on the Rue des Putains. The coin and note were discovered while his body was being prepared for shipment back to his manor.

THE JUDGMENT OF THE GODS | 71

"The third incident involved Monsignor Lezay, an advisor to His Holiness, who was beaten to death on the Rue Fortunée. Count Boson was hit on the head while walking through Avignon."

"All of these deaths occurred in town?" my master said.

"Indeed," Father Arlan said.

"Well, then," Father William said, "if three of the victims resided outside Avignon, how did the killer know their schedules while they were here?"

The other two exchanged glances and shrugged. They had no idea.

"Where was the demand note left?" Father Occam asked.

"In the alms box of the cathedral," Johad said.

My master rubbed his chin and frowned.

"Which of the bodies were sent home for burial?" he asked.

"All but Lezay's," came the reply, "which was interred at the Monastery of Saint Herbin."

"Then that's the one we shall exhume," Father William said, "on the morrow, if you please."

"It shall be done, Father Occam," Johad said.

After the two priests departed, my master put the implements in his purse, and indicated on our way out that we would make another stop.

"There is a man," he said, "who may be able to tell us something about these artifacts."

We wound our way down a number of narrow streets into an older section of town, finally entering the Rue David.

"What is this place?" I asked, looking at a curiously-shaped emblem of a star embedded on one door.

"The Jewish quarter," he said, knocking on the small round window of an adjoining building.

"Yesss?" someone said within.

"Occamus Magus to see Master Yehuda ben Sion," my teacher said.

"One moment."

Then the door cracked open, and a short, middle-aged man

with a long, graying beard peeped out. He wore a red skullcap pressed into his straggly black hair.

"Come in, come in!" he cackled. "How good to see you again, Frère Occam."

He gave my master a kiss on both cheeks, and then beckoned us inside.

The shop, for such it was, was strangely outfitted. On one wall hung the dried skins, heads, and entrails of mostly unidentifiable animals. On another I saw jars of roots and herbs and powders and other such things. On the third were large crystals and curiously-shaped jewels and twisted silver implements. On the fourth were hung various garments and hats, all of them oddly cut and decorated. I could smell incense burning somewhere, but couldn't place the fragrance.

The Jew took us back into a second room, obviously his workshop, with a long table set against one wall. We perched ourselves on several wooden chairs.

"What can I do for you, my friend?" Yehuda asked.

Father William removed the four coins from his pouch, and laid them on the table. The shopkeeper pulled out an oblong piece of cut glass from a drawer, and ran it over the artifacts, moving the thing back and forth as he peered at them.

"What is that?" I asked.

"It makes my vision wax stronger," the man said. "You will understand, my boy, when you get older.

"These are very unusual pieces, very old, ben Occam. The lettering is Greek, but of a style I have never encountered before. These dots on the back, very curious indeed. The inscription reads, 'Vasileós Philippou Epiphanous Philadelphou,' or in your tongue, 'From the King Philip,' the, uh, how do you say? 'coming-to-light,' no, the better word is 'famous,' 'the one who is devoted to his brother.' I have seen a similar coin of the great King Alexander; I know that his father was named Philip, and also his half-brother, so perhaps it is one of these. I will make the usual inquiries for you, f I may retain these for a day or two."

"Of course," my friend said, discretely leaving a copper on

THE JUDGMENT OF THE GODS | 73

the bench.

"Thank you, ben Occam," ben Sion said, "you are very good to me."

"No more than you deserve, old soul."

Then they kissed again, and we headed back to the abbey.

"Who was that?" I asked my teacher.

"An acquaintance from my Oxford days," he said. "He did me a favor once, and when the pogrom of '07 threatened his family, I ensured their safe passage out of the country."

"But he must be a magician," I said. "If the authorities knew...."

"They know!" Occam sighed. "They tolerate him and his countrymen, because they provide services no one else would render.

"Now," he said, "we need to examine the facts of this case. Four men have been killed, all of them with ties to Papa John. We must ask the obvious question, *cui bono?*—that is, whose benefit would be served by the resignation or disgrace of the pontiff?"

"There are many such possibilities," I said, "including the remnants of the Templars and those other religious orders who have been attacked by this pope and his predecessor, Papa Clemens."

"There may also be personal reasons involved," my master said, "such as revenge, greed, lust for power. All of these things may prompt a man to murder. We know too little at this point to speculate overmuch. Tomorrow we must begin looking into the crimes themselves. Let us pray to God for guidance, that He will show us the way."

And so we knelt down on that hard stone floor, lending our muted voices to the Lord, and then went off to bed.

* * * * * * *

IN THE MORNING we joined the pontiff's two aides at Saint Herbin's Abbey, just outside the city walls, where two workmen had already begun excavating the tomb of Monsignor Lezay. Soon they reached the coffin, and employed ropes to haul it out of the ground.

"Ooh!" one of them exclaimed, when the lid came off.

The stench was overpowering, and I ran behind an adjoining monument to void my breakfast.

Father William, however, merely tied a rag around his nose, and began poking and prodding the remains. At one point he even asked the laborers to rotate the corpse, while I looked on from a distance—a great distance!

Then he was finished, and exchanged a few words with the two priests, before motioning me to follow.

"What did you find?" I asked.

"He was indeed beaten before he died, although whether those injuries actually caused his death, I cannot tell. There was a crude cross cut into his chest. Similar marks were apparently found on the other bodies as well, in one case etched into the forehead."

"What does it mean?" I asked.

"The murderer wants us to think that the Templars were responsible," Occam said. "But these scratches are not firm evidence of any such connection."

"Where do we go next?"

"We look into the background of Lezay, and the circumstances of his passing."

Already he was hurrying out of the cemetery.

"Come, Thaddæus," he shouted, "time's a-wasting."

On the Rue Fortunée in the Bélon District, we began questioning residents, shop men, even passersby, about the crime.

"I knowed this Lezay," an apothecary named Rocambole said, "he come here often to buy his powders. But we was closed when he was killed. It's just not safe staying open after dark."

"When was the last time you saw him?" my master said.

"Well, let me see," the proprietor said, "you knows, I think it was the same day that he died. He was with another man. Now that I think about it, there was something strange about the companion. Oh yes, I remember: he was dressed as a working man, yet I caught a glimpse of the pectoral cross on his chest, and he talked and acted just like a clergyman. You see a lot of people in my business, and you get so's you can pick them out, if you knows what I mean."

"What did they discuss?" Father William asked.

"Can't say that I really paid that much attention," Rocambole said, "except...well, they had an argument just as they were leaving. The other man, he said to Lezay, 'You'll do it!' and the monsignor, he kept shaking his head, 'No.' That's all I know."

As we left the shopkeeper's establishment, we brushed by a man entering the place, and he abruptly pressed something into my left hand. I turned to give it back, but Father William grabbed the elbow of my right arm and muscled me out into the street. We marched another block before he asked me to show him the thing. It was a small, rolled scrap of paper, which, when unraveled, said, "*Vendidit hic auro patriam*," or, "This man sold his country for gold."

"Now *that's* very interesting," was all that my master would say, before stuffing the message in his purse.

That afternoon we visited Saint Jude's Church, and spoke to the priest there, Father Ursus, a florid man in his mid-thirties. He told us that Bishop Thoune had been staying with him during his visit to Avignon.

"What was his business with the pope?" Father William asked.

"I'd rather not say," the pudgy priest said.

"I have the authority of the Holy Father in this matter," my master said. "If you wish, I can get confirmation from the papal offices."

"No, that won't be necessary. I think it had something to do with your order, actually."

"Indeed?"

"Yes, Bishop Thoune was reporting on the activities of Michael de Cesena, your Father General, operating under the pope's direct instructions," the priest said.

"The Holy Father asked the bishop to spy on our leader?" I said.

"Well, yes," he said.

"Why?" Father William asked.

"As you know, Cesena has been criticized for stating that Jesus and his followers owned no property of their own, thereby implying that the Catholic Church and its clergy should follow His example. These views have been deemed heretical by Papa John and his cardinals, and so the pope asked Bishop Thoune to, shall we say, watch over the Father General."

"Do you know what he was going to recommend to Papa John?"

"No," the priest said. "He died the day before his audience, and never told me."

He knew nothing else. My master thanked the priest, and we returned to Saint Anaclète's for supper and prayers.

* * * * * * *

WE FOUND OUR way back to the Jewish shopkeeper the next morning.

"Ah, my very good friend, I have news for you," he said, dragging us back into his workroom. "These silver coins, they show the image of King Philip of Syria, surnamed Philadelphus, who died about 1,400 years ago."

"Before the time of Christ," my master said.

"As you say," Yehuda replied. "But there is something very interesting about these pieces. When the Romans annexed Syria, twenty years after Philip's death, they kept on minting these coins for another fifty years or so, using the same images. They called them tetradrachms, and they were widely employed by the moneychangers."

"How strange to keep a dead king's face on a Roman coin," Father William said. "They were common?"

"In Syria, Israel, Mesopotamia," came the response. "Common then, uncommon now."

THE JUDGMENT OF THE GODS | 77

The shopkeeper reluctantly handed the four coins back to Father Occam, and then added: "I've heard that the Emperor Ludwig will soon name his own pope."

"Making a pope and having him accepted are two different things," Father William noted. "Thank you, old friend."

We were heading back to the center of town when a papal guard approached us.

"You Father Occam?" he asked.

When my master nodded, the soldier ordered, "Come at once."

We followed him to the Papal Palace, where we were immediately taken to the pope.

"Father Johad is dead!" he gasped, holding out his palm.

On it was a fifth coin, cousin to the other pieces in our possession, and a scrap of papyrus labeled with the number v.

Father William took both pieces, and put them in his purse with the rest.

"Arlan!" the pope yelled quite loudly, and the aide came rushing into the chamber.

"Yes, Holiness," d'Esprit said.

"I want them arrested," came the order, "Jews, gypsies, former members of the Templars, the leaders of the other militant orders, all of them. I want them interned by sunset. Round up the usual suspects, and then begin the interrogations at once."

When Father Arlan failed to respond as quickly as the pontiff desired, John shouted: "*Now!* Or you'll be added to the list yourself."

"As you say, Holiness," the aide said, hurrying from the room.

"Where are my murderers, Occam?" the pope asked.

"I'll have them for you within the week," my master said, "but first I must view the body of Father Johad."

"Oh, very well," the pontiff said. "Get out! Get out now!"

"I've never seen him like this," Arlan said, motioning to us frantically as we exited the room. "He's going to do himself an injury."

The priest led us to the adjoining cathedral, and thence to a side altar. The body of Johad le Physe sprawled next to a prie-Dieu. A papal guard stood at attention nearby.

"He's not been moved?" Father William asked.

"No," Arlan said, "save to inspect his mouth."

My master motioned me to approach. Father Johad's head was lying in a pool of congealed blood. His throat had been sliced.

"What strikes you about this scene?" Father Occam asked me.

"There's no sign of a struggle, sir," I said.

"Thus?"

"He either knew his attacker and wasn't afraid of him, or didn't hear him approach."

"Walk over there twenty paces," my master said, "and then back again."

As I did so, my sandals made a clop-clop-clop sound on the hard stone floor. But when I removed them, and tried again, there was very little racket.

"I've seen enough," Father William said.

Then he turned to the aide: "I would like a pass to the dungeons."

"Whatever for?" Father Arlan said.

"I want to visit someone there," my master said.

Then we departed.

* * * * * * *

THAT AFTERNOON, we visited a certain Madame Joyaue on the Rue des Putains. I had never been to this kind of establishment before, and was abashed by the accouterments. Several of the female denizens made rude remarks.

"Ignore them," Father William said, before we were escorted back to the owner's private office.

"We don't see too many monks here," Joyaue said. "Bishops, yes, even some cardinals on occasion, but not your sort."

"We haven't any money," came the laconic reply.

"Maybe that's why. What do you want, father?"

"Sieur Phocion, cousin of His Holiness," Father Occam said.

"We don't use names here," the madame said.

"He was murdered here last month," my master stated, "stabbed, I believe."

"Why should I tell you anything?"

"Because I carry the pope's authority," he said, "and if you don't, I'll have you expelled from Avignon."

"Oh, very well," Joyaue said. "He was a guest during his visit to our fair city. Of course, we gave him every consideration."

"Of course."

"Amalie found him with a knife in his back."

My master was puzzled. "But aren't the activities here usually carried out with the joint participation of both parties?"

"He liked to watch."

"What?" I asked.

"He liked to watch other people being, umm, active, as you say. From an adjoining room, peering through a peephole."

"Oh."

"Who else was present then?" Father William asked.

"I have no idea. You think we keep a roster here? Ha!"

"Is there any other way into your establishment except the front?"

"Of course," she said. "The demoiselles enter through the back door, and there's also an escape route in case we're raided."

"Then anyone could have come and gone unannounced and unnoticed," my master said.

We thanked the proprietress for her assistance, and returned to the abbey.

* * * * * * *

THAT EVENING, WE visited the dungeons beneath the civil palace in the center of town, after collecting our passes from the papal chancellery.

Father William first sought out the cell of Yehuda ben Sion.

"I'm sorry, old friend," he said.

"It's those coins," the Jew said, "they're accursed."

"How?" my master asked.

"They have a stink about them," the shopkeeper said. "You have the implements. Look for yourself, and you shall see."

Then he retreated into himself, moaning about his fate.

Father Occam next asked the guards to show us the supposed Templars, all six of them, but when he saw them, indicated that he would speak with just one. We waited until the prisoner was isolated before introducing ourselves.

"I know you," the middle-aged man said.

There was something familiar about the voice. Then it came to me: it was the Grand Master of the Hidden Temple, the masked individual with whom we had dealt a year earlier, when we'd been loaned the Holy Shroud.

"I know *you!*" I said, and whispered the particulars in my master's ear.

"I thought so," Father Occam said.

"Perhaps you already know too much," the Templar said.

"On the contrary," Father William said. "Abide me most carefully, good sir. I must have answers that only you can supply, or we may all soon find ourselves in very warm circumstances."

"I cannot reveal any secrets which are bound by oath," the grand master said.

"Then tell me whatever you can. Did you or your brethren have anything to do with these murders?"

"No."

"Do you know who perpetrated these crimes?"

"No."

"A year ago, you gave us the Shroud, for which the Templar Order was acting as custodian," Father William said. "But you also mentioned other ancient 'treasures' that had been removed from Acre before that city fell to the Muslims in '92. Is that correct?"

There was a pause while the man considered his response.

"Yes," he finally said.

THE JUDGMENT OF THE GODS | 81

"Were any of these taken by Papa Clemens and King Philip le Bel when they attacked the Templars in '07?"

Another hesitation, another reluctant, "Yes."

"Can you tell me anything about these artifacts?"

"Not unless you uncover them first," the Templar said. "Be very careful, Father Occam. If handled incorrectly, even the Shroud of Our Lord can have a most potent effect on those whose hearts are not pure."

"Thank you for your forbearance," Father Occam said. "May God bless both you and your order."

"And you also," came the reply.

When we were leaving, I asked my master if he knew who the Templar really was.

"His secular name?" Father William said. "I choose not to investigate such matters. Sometimes, friend Thaddæus, it is better to be ignorant of certain realities."

I pondered this response all the way back to the monastery.

* * * * * * *

THE NEXT MORNING, we sought out Father Arlan again, to gain further insight into the pope's late cousin, Count Boson.

"According to Father Johad's notes," the priest said, "Boson had been delegated the task of investigating the murders, and had reported to Papa Jean that an underground remnant of the Templars was at fault. However, although he had the name of a man he thought was involved in the plot, he wanted to capture the leaders, and so asked permission to continue the search. The pope agreed."

"Do you have any record regarding the suspect's identity?" my master asked.

"Boson just called him 'le prêtre,' or 'the priest'."

"What about the count's background?" Friar Occam asked. "What can you tell us?"

D'Esprit thought for a moment. "Boson honorably served both the king and the pope, the latter from his accession nine years ago."

"The king in question was the late Philip IV?"

"Yes, the very one who suppressed the Templars. Actually, now that I think about it, I believe that the count reported directly to Minister Nogaret during those years."

"Ah," was Father William's only comment. "How long did Boson work for the king?"

"I don't know exactly, sir. He did tell me in March that his service for the pope now exceeded his time with King Philip, so perhaps eight or nine years."

"When did Pope John ask him to investigate these murders?"

"Why, from the very first case. He was present, you know, when Bishop Thoune died, and so it was only natural that the pontiff would request his assistance, him being a relative and all."

My master pondered this, and then said: "Relate to me the circumstances of Count Boson's passing."

"He had taken a six-squad of papal guards, as he had done several times before, to arrest someone in the Tournal District," Father Arlan said. "Father Johad's notes do not indicate specifically who was implicated. The body of the count and his men were found in a crumbling house on the Rue des Chèvres, partially buried under a wall that had collapsed onto them."

"I thought there was some kind of deviltry at work," Father William said.

"There were strange markings chalked on one of the intact walls of the structure."

"Nothing else?"

"No."

"Very well," my master said. "Thank you for your help."

But as we turned to go, he stopped and spoke again: "One additional question, if you please. Father Johad was a Blaisean. What about Bishop Thoune and Monsignor Lezay?"

"Dominicans, both," the priest replied.

As we walked back through the city to the monastery, I said, "I don't understand why the clerics' affiliations should be

THE JUDGMENT OF THE GODS | 83

important."

"They are and they aren't," he said, "depending on one's perspective."

His answer didn't much elucidate matters.

When we reached our cells, Father William directed me to pack up the Holy Shroud and the ancient speculum. I asked him where we were going, and he just said, "Tournal."

The latter section of Avignon was dirty and mean, being occupied by the lowest level of the social stratum. Even so, the grim men existing there quickly gave way before the equally grave mien of Friar Occam, and we had only to question two of the natives before being directed to the place where Count Boson had perished. We pulled open the worn wooden door of the house, and carefully entered the decaying structure.

"Pull the Shroud over your shoulders, Thaddæus," he said, and I complied. We could see dried brown patches on some of the fallen bricks.

Father William gave me the speculum and lit a candle. The implement was round in shape and polished to a supernally bright sheen, looking almost green at times. I could not read the runes inscribed on its back. He had me sit in the dirt with my legs crossed under my body, the speculum held upright with its convex side towards me. Then he propped the light upright on a brick a few feet away, gradually adjusting its length to and fro until he reached the proper distance.

"Hold steady now," he said, and mumbled a few words under his breath.

Suddenly I felt the metal vibrate between my hands, and the candlelight seemed to concentrate right at the center of the device, throwing a beam of bright light towards the place where the wall had once stood. Then the bricks jumped from the floor into their former places again—my master whispered in my ear, "Neither speak nor move, Thaddæus"—and I witnessed the ghostly images of seven men fighting with an eighth, all falling down when the wall shook and tumbled 'round them. Then the becloaked image of a ninth individual entered the room, exam-

84 | ROBERT REGINALD

ined the scene, and exited.

I gasped and the light vanished, the speculum tumbling from my limp hands.

"Are you all right?" Father William asked.

"Yes," I managed to say, "just give me a moment. What was that?"

"An image out of the past," he said. "And now, I think, I know enough."

We packed the magical implement and Shroud back in their cases, and I strapped the packs onto my back.

I was surprised to see the light so dim when we finally exited the ruined house.

"How long have we been inside?" I asked.

"Long enough," my master said.

As we emerged from the alley, a large man suddenly blocked our way, and I heard the rustling of other steps just behind us.

"What mischief is this?" Friar Occam shouted.

"Your death," the man said, pulling out a knife.

The ruffian lashed out with the edge of the blade, but Father William hit him with his hand, and the stiletto went bouncing away into the gutter.

"Damn you," the man shouted, reaching out with his two large hands. Behind me someone grabbed my shoulder. There was a bright flash and a scream. I heard a shout of "My hand! My hand!"—and then the thud of someone falling.

I briefly turned around, but a third attacker was already fleeing, and the one who had accosted me was holding his burned limb, rolling and moaning in the muck of the alleyway. The first man was still lashing out at Father William, but then he too fell to the ground, unconscious. My master quickly searched him, and pulled from his purse a sixth coin and a scrap of parchment marked VI.

"Voilà!" he said.

Then we went home to Saint Anaclète's, where I secured the Shroud in its resting place. Friar Occam sent a note to the papal chancellery, requesting a meeting with the pontiff on the morrow. Then he went out by himself for a few hours, while I fell into bed, totally exhausted. I think he returned in the early evening.

* * * * * * *

POPE JOHN XXII was his usual acerbic self, being flanked on this occasion by his new chief assistant, Father Arlan, and several of the papal guards.

"Well, what do you have?" he asked.

"You asked me, Holiness, to investigate the murder of your nephew, Count Boson, and several other individuals associated with you," Friar Occam said.

"Yes? Yes?"

"I have some answers for you, which you may or may not wish to hear," my master continued, "but first, you must give me your solemn promise that you will immediately release any of those arrested by your guards this past week who are innocent of these crimes."

"Perhaps they're guilty of something else," the pontiff said.

"Perhaps we're all guilty of something in the eyes of the Lord," Father William said, "but that is for God to decide, not man. You will release them, or I will tell you nothing."

"Very well," Papa John reluctantly agreed. "I do so promise. All of the prisoners except those actually charged with these crimes shall be freed by sunset today."

My master nodded his head, and thought for a moment how best to begin his presentation.

"This puzzle has been one of the most difficult that I have yet encountered," he said, "involving five victims, or eleven if we count your guards, and several murderers."

"Several?" the pope asked.

"Indeed," Father William said, "and we must examine each crime separately to arrive at the best possible solution.

"First, we have Bishop Thoune, who mysteriously choked to death at a dinner given in his honor at Saint Jude's Church.

Curiously, at least one other victim, Count Boson, attended this celebration. Who else was present at this function, Father Arlan?"

The priest was taken aback by this sudden interrogatory.

"W-well," he stammered, "I think Monsignor Lezay was there, and perhaps Father Johad, too."

"Bishop Thoune choked on something. What happened then?"

"We all rushed to help him, and someone called for a physician. It was chaos, utter chaos," the aide said.

"Think carefully, now. Who reached the body first?"

"Uh, well, it was Monsignor Lezay," Arlan said.

"Who else gathered with him around the *corpus*?" Father William said.

"I think...well, Count Boson, myself, Father Johad, Sieur Phocion...why, they're all dead, all except me!"

"Yes," my master said, "all of the future victims were present. We know that Thoune was poisoned, and the pertinent question, of course, is why. Holiness, I believe that you had given him a task to undertake on your behalf."

"He was asked to monitor the political activities of Father General Cesena," the pontiff said.

"Indeed," my master said, "and this initially misled me, as I briefly considered the possibility that a Franciscan had been responsible for the bishop's murder. Thoune might have been preparing to report something scurrilous about the order at the audience with you scheduled for the very next day. But then I considered the reality of the situation: what could he possibly have learned about Cesena that wasn't already general knowledge? The Father Superior is a public figure; his opinions are well known.

"No, it had to be something else, something potentially dire to one or more of the individuals already present at the dinner. I think that Bishop Thoune accidentally uncovered someone in your entourage, Holiness, who was selling information about the papal court to a third party, possibly the Emperor Ludwig, your avowed enemy."

"What!" the pope exclaimed. "This is preposterous! Who could it be?"

"Actually, it was Monsignor Lezay," Father William said.

"But he was one of the victims," I said, unable to contain myself.

"Indeed," my master said, "but that in itself is not an impediment. We have just heard how the monsignor was the first person to reach Thoune. I had already noticed that the parchment taken from the bishop's mouth was the only one not discolored by saliva. Lezay displayed to his frantic audience the scrap and coin that he had supposedly removed from his victim's lips, but they had never actually been there."

"Yes, he was the one who found them," d'Esprit said.

"Also, I discovered yesterday that Lezay's background is completely unknown. I researched him in the Papal Archives, but found nothing in his file beyond the date that he first joined the Dominicans, less than a year after the dissolution of the Templars. I could tell by the creases in the folder that many more documents had once been included there, but everything else had been removed. I suspect that as a young man Lezay had joined the Templars, perhaps as a squire. When King Philip attacked in '07, he escaped by changing his name and affiliation, as did so many others."

"I knew the Templars were involved!" the pope said.

"Philip's nefarious minister, Nogaret, coordinated the assault on the temples. Their goal was the seizure of the vaunted Templar treasure, which we now know consisted mainly of various religious artifacts from the time of Christ, which have little monetary value. But was the Shroud the Templars' entire trove? I think not. I believe that Nogaret found something else in the Paris Temple, and gave it to the king, who perished along with Papa Clemens in 1314, just months after they had burned Jacques de Molay.

"Somehow, this confiscated treasure found its way back into a collection of church documents and materials relating to the

88 | ROBERT REGINALD

Templars. Naturally, when Lezay joined the Papal Chancellery, he became curious about the risk that its files might pose to him, and so he investigated the documents and purged his own. At the same time, he found something completely unexpected in the archives— part of the Templar treasure—and he removed it.

"And then, when he realized last month that Thoune's pending report to the pope posed a direct threat to himself, he killed the bishop, using one of the powders that he purchased from an apothecary on the Rue Fortunée. Someone at that shop, another phantom murderer, gave me a slip of paper that said, '*Vendidit hic auro patriam*,' or, 'This man sold his country for gold,' in a blatant attempt to throw suspicion on Lezay, but it was nothing but the truth.

"Lezay himself used an artifact from the Templar treasure to place blame on the long-suppressed order, thinking that someone from the old regime might well recognize the piece. His ploy proved more successful than he ever could have anticipated.

"Count Boson was also present at the dinner for Bishop Thoune. Boson had been a runner for Nogaret in his early years, and had seen the coins then, perhaps even handled them. He immediately recognized the one from Thoune's mouth, and asked you, Holiness, to allow him to investigate the crime, which he believed was connected to the Templars."

"Then, why was Sieur Phocion killed?" the pontiff asked.

"That puzzled me for a long time," Father William said, "but I finally decided that Lezay murdered him merely to throw Boson off the scent. Two such deaths, plus a demand that Your Holiness resign, constituted a major conspiracy against the papacy, instead of something accomplished primarily for personal benefit."

"Then who killed Lezay?" Father Arlan asked.

"Count Boson, of course. He was a better investigator than anyone knew, including himself. He suspected everyone, not just the Templars, and had Lezay's quarters secretly searched. Of course, as soon as he found the artifacts, he knew the name of the killer. He decided to pressure Lezay into revealing his accomplices, but the man proved obstinate. The beating perhaps went too far, and then the count was left with a body to hide. Thus, he maintained the fiction of a Templar conspiracy by putting another of the coins into Lezay's mouth.

"However, Lezay's partner and fellow spy wasn't sure whether or not his friend had betrayed him, and so he lured Boson and his men into a trap, rigging an old wall to collapse upon them. He stole the coins, and continued the fiction of a Templar conspiracy."

"What about Father Johad?" the pontiff asked.

"He was beginning to ask uncomfortable questions about Count Boson's investigation, having inherited the man's notes, and came to believe, or at least hint, that something about the scenario was just not right. He communicated that suspicion to the wrong person, thereby signing his own death warrant."

"And who was this accomplice?" Father d'Esprit said.

"Why, that would be you!" my master said. "Father Johad knew his murderer intimately, and never felt any anxiety about being alone with him. It was, I might add, a serious lapse of judgment."

"Seize him!" the pontiff ordered.

"But...but....," the man sputtered, as the guards grabbed his arms and hauled him away.

"He will reveal everything by the time my interrogators have finished with him. Now, then, Father Occam, what exactly was this treasure?" the pope asked.

"The thirty pieces of silver paid to Judas Iscariot for the betrayal of Our Lord Jesus Christ," Father William said. "It taints everyone who touches it, being accursed by God for all time. The Templars found the cache in Jerusalem, and hid it away from the world, hoping to limit its influence, but it destroyed them in the end, as it destroyed King Philip, Pope Clement, Monsignor Lezay, Father Arlan, and many, many others. I will search d'Esprit's possessions and find the coins, and then secrete the treasure somewhere safe. With Your Holiness's permission, of course."

"As you say," he ordered. "Now go and leave me in peace, Friar Occam."

"And the prisoners?" my master said.

"They will be released this afternoon, as promised," the pontiff said, clearly displeased at his hand being forced. "This audience is over."

* * * * * * *

"WHAT WILL YOU do with them?" Father William asked.

We were talking with the Grand Master of the Templar Order, who had never given us his name, knowing that it was safer for us both if we did not know.

Laid out on a table in front of us were thirty shiny tetradrachms of King Philip Philadelphus, looking as new as the day they had been minted. He slowly put them into a leather satchel, and frowned.

"When we left Acre for the last time in '92, after the Muslims had taken the Holy Land," he said, "one of our brethren dumped the coins into the sea, thinking that the curse of the thirty pieces of silver had destroyed our final strongholds in Palestine. Several months later a fisherman on Cyprus cut open the belly of a shark and found the trove. After being plagued with continual ill luck, he donated the lot to the Templars.

"We cannot give them away, knowing what they will do to others. They cannot be lost or discarded, without returning to us again. So, I do not have an answer to your question."

"Perhaps I can offer a solution," my master said.

He motioned me to come forward. I was once again carrying the Holy Shroud of Our Lord Jesus Christ. I removed the cloth, and wrapped it carefully around my right hand and arm. Then I leaned forward and picked up one of the coins out of its container.

I felt a surge of energy, and heard a sizzling sound as the metal began to pop and melt and boil away. Thirty times I accom-

THE JUDGMENT OF THE GODS | 91

plished this deed. Thirty times we said a prayer for the repose of the souls of those who had been tainted by these accursed coins.

When the last of them was gone, I carefully folded up the Shroud, and handed it back to the leader of the Templar Order.

"I believe this is yours, sir," I said.

"I believe you're right," he said, smiling at us for the very first time.

OCCAM'S MEASURE

She was a slim, dark figure enshrouded in a plain black robe, her only ornament a small crucifix enchained around her slender neck. Her simple sandals clip-clopped along the tired cobblestones of the Rue de __—she knew not what, nor did she care. It might as well have been the Rue de la Boue—the Way of Mud—because that's what she was slogging through—that and the human and animal waste that guttered down the middle of the street.

Her name was Sœur Astrée, and she was an acolyte of the Monastery of Sainte-Énimie. And on this early evening of mid-September 1325, she was tired and hungry and eager to get back to the small comforts of the convent where she'd spent the last five years of her life.

Mother Marie-Alice had sent her across town to take some buckbean to the wife of Baron Poncin, whose digestion was poorly; but instead of being able to return immediately, as she had hoped, she'd had to remain to show the cook how to prepare the herb properly and administer it to the patient. And now the shadows were gathering, and the wind was winding its hasty way off the Rhône up through the alleys of Avignon.

She shuddered and pulled her robe around her more tightly, trying to keep the chill off her narrow shoulders.

There were few residents out and about at this time of day—it was too late for the merchants and peddlers, and too early for the ladies of the night. Astrée turned a corner onto Cobblers' Lane, and nearly ran head-on into a man coming from the opposite direction.

"*Pardon*, Sister," he said, glancing back at the street behind him. "I appear to be…uh, lost. Can you tell me how to find the Chapel of…uh, Saint-Maixent?"

"Why, it's back the way you came, monsieur," she said.

"Well, how very silly of me," he said, smiling crookedly. He had a slight accent. "Could you possibly show me the way, if you please?"

Astrée really didn't want to take the time—she was just so late already—but Sister Luette was always telling them that they had to do charity in their lives, and here was something that she could do to help this stranger.

So she led him the six blocks through a series of increasingly narrow alleys to the nearly ruined visage of the chapel, set far back away from the street, finally saying, "This is it, monsieur!"

That was the last thing that she ever said in this world, although she did have a moment to consider, as the cord tightened around her neck, that life was exceedingly unfair, when all she'd been trying to do was to practice some loving-kindness to others.

* * * * * * *

OUR VISITOR TAPPED very lightly on the back door of our cottage, just after sunset on Michaelmas Eve, and when I opened it, I saw there a tall, ascetic man of perhaps fifty years. He was clean-shaven and wore the black robes of a Benedictine monk.

"Father Seraphim to see Doctor William," the man whispered—and only by his muted voice did I finally recognize him. It was Father Michael de Cesena, Superior-General of the Order of the Friars Minor.

I quickly motioned him inside and closed the door.

"Who is it?" Master William asked.

"Perhaps you should see for yourself, sir," I said, leading our guest into the front room.

"Michael!" Father William said. After rising from his seat

94 | ROBERT REGINALD

and embracing his friend, he just shook his head. "If Pope John discovers your presence in Avignon, he'll have you arrested, condemned, and flambéed within the month."

"It was important that I talk to you, William," the Franciscan leader said. "Things are starting to get serious out there, and I badly need some of that level-headed advice that you're so famous for. But, why are you living *here*? I thought you were lodged at Saint Anaclète's."

"So we were until a few months ago, and then the Holy Father decided that he could keep better track of us in a separate facility. You'll find our faithful hounds out front, lurking by both day and night. However, they pay little attention to the small garden in the rear."

"I had to climb the back wall to reach you," Cesena said. "Fortunately, I had good directions."

"What's this all about?" my master asked.

Cesena sighed. "As you know, William, Emperor Ludwig trounced his chief political rival on the battlefield earlier this year, and made Duke Friedrich his prisoner. Since then, Ludwig has sought the pope's ratification of his election as the Roman King, but John has thus far refused. Now, the Emperor is beginning to consider other alternatives."

"*What* other alternatives?"

"If necessary, the election of a new pope, although he hopes that it won't come to that."

"*A new pontiff?*" My master seemed perplexed at the idea. "Who among the cardinals supports such a move?"

"Well, none, so far."

"Without that support, Michael, your effort's doomed before it begins. We've had too many would-be popes in the past who lacked legitimacy…."

We were suddenly interrupted by a "boom-boom-boom" on the front door. "Open, in the name of Papa Johannes!" came the faint command.

"My God, it's the Pope's Noses!" Cesena hissed. "They know I'm here! It's the end for all of us!"

THE JUDGMENT OF THE GODS | 95

"Sssh," my master said. "Put him in the vegetable bin, Thaddæus."

"Yes, sir," I said, and led our visitor to a wooden box in the back room. I moved a table, lifted up the floor board, and indicated an empty space that hollowed back under the container. "It's a tight fit," I said, "but better than the alternative."

Cesena slid into the hole without a murmur of protest.

Then I closed the lid, rushed to the main entrance, and opened the door.

A squad of Papal soldiers stood outside.

"We have a summons," their captain said, "For Father William of Occam. He's to appear before His Holiness without delay."

"We're ready to leave now, sir," my master said, from somewhere behind me. He indicated that I should follow him.

* * * * * * *

AT THE PALAIS des Papes, we were left waiting for some time before His Holiness Pope John XXII finally summoned us. For the past month, he'd been entertaining a delegation from the Ecumenical Patriarch Isaias I, and had found the easterners difficult to please—or so the rumors went.

Finally, we were led to the small Papal audience room called "Fabulosus" (renowned) by the pontiff, but "Fabalis" (beans) by the Avignonese, with their mordant sense of humor.

The leader of the western Christian world looked uncommonly grim and bowed down with cares (he was then about seventy-six years of age). He motioned us to be seated. Then he dismissed all of his aides save Bishop Polyphème Écorchure, who'd taken the place of Father d'Esprit, the late and unlamented murderer.

"Fra William," Pope John said.

"I give thanks to the Lord for your continued good health, Holiness," my teacher said.

"Never mind that. *My great-niece is dead!*" the pontiff said, his voice trembling. "She was my favorite of all the family—sweet, pretty, intelligent, and utterly devoted to God. She would have been an abbess had she lived."

"I'm truly sorry to hear this news," Father William said. "You have my...."

The pope waved him to silence. "She was *murdered*, Occam!" John said.

"Murdered? Are you quite certain?"

"She was murdered!—violated, strangled with a cord, and then butchered into pieces like some domestic animal! I've seen many evil things in my day, Father William, but this...this is by far the worst, and not just because she was so dear to me."

"But...but...I've heard nothing of this," my teacher said.

"We've suppressed the news to avoid panic," the pope said. He sighed, very loud and very long. "But it's even worse than that: four other nuns have been killed this past month, all in the same way. My soldiers have been unable to stop this fiend.

"Find this man, Occam! Find him now! Do whatever's necessary to end this! Écorchure will provide you with whatever you need. You have my authority to conduct your investigation"—he removed a signet ring from his finger and handed it to the bishop.

"You must move quickly. If word spreads into the general population, there'll be riots in the city, and people will say that the Pope evem can't stop the Devil from entering his own home."

He leaned forward on his throne. "I shan't rest until the man who violated my dear niece has been brought to a swift and sure justice. *Do you understand?*"

"I do, Holiness," said my master.

Just then, a priest entered from a side door, hurried over to the Pope, and whispered something in his ear.

"Now?" the pontiff almost yelled, obviously irritated. "He wants *what*?"

Before any of us could react, a strangely garbed clergyman burst from the same entrance, shouting at the leader of the

THE JUDGMENT OF THE GODS | 97

Western church: "This is outrageous, Eminence! My master will not tolerate such treatment!"

"What is it now, Father Gennadios?" the Pope said, struggling with difficulty to maintain his dignity and calm.

"It's the 'Filioque' again. We've been asked to…."

"Bishop Écorchure will be happy to address this issue, and find some solution for you. Is there anything *else*, sir?"

The Eastern churchman suddenly noticed us sitting there for the first time. "Oh, have I interrupted a meeting or something? Well, I do apologize most profusely, Patriarch John."

"Please employ my proper title when addressing me," the pontiff said.

Then he nodded towards us: "Father William, you may leave us now."

The bishop escorted us into the hallway. "If you'll let me know your requirements first thing tomorrow, I'll be happy to provide you with whatever you need. In the meantime, I must go…."

We returned to our cottage near the river, *sans* our escort, where we found Father Michael waiting for us. He'd found his way out of temporary confinement, it seemed.

"You're still here?" Father William asked his old friend. "You must leave before you're discovered, Michael."

"Not until I have your answer," Cesena said.

"*What* answer?"

"I've been approached by a representative of Emperor Ludwig. He wants to know if the Franciscans will support the deposition of John and the appointment of a replacement. So I'm polling the most influential members of our Order."

"No," said my teacher, shaking his head to emphasize his refusal.

"But…why?"

"I've given my oath not to leave Avignon until released by the pope; I take such promises quite seriously. Also, without building a political and religious foundation for a new papacy, you have no possibility of succeeding.

"The man's in his mid-seventies—how many more years does he have? Let God choose the time of his passing, and try in the meantime to groom a successor who has some realistic chance of being elected in his place."

"He wants to remove me," Father Michael said.

"Then he can remove you—he has that authority. If this issue becomes just about you or Ludwig, then you're both doomed."

"You won't support us, then?"

"Not under the present circumstances," Master William said.

"Very well. This isn't the end of this, you know."

"I hardly thought so. Go with God, Michael—and do please be careful!"

"You, too, old friend."

I checked out back to make certain no one was watching, and then helped the monk over the wall. The last that I saw of him was a shadow oozing away into the night.

* * * * * * *

THE NEXT MORNING, we met Bishop Écorchure at the Palace, who introduced us to several others. Officer Houdain had been conducting the investigation of the murders. There were also a physician named Doctor Martial, Mother Méraudine of the Sisters of Plentiful Sorrow, and Sister Sassica of the same order.

"Five nuns have been brutally murdered," Houdain said, "one per week beginning the last week of August."

"When specifically did the first death occur?" my master asked.

"On the feast of Saint Bartholomew, sir, thirty-six days ago."

"What about the others?"

According to the officer, their deaths had occurred anywhere from six to eight days apart, with no obvious pattern between them.

"The last murder was six days ago," Father William said. "So, the next killing must be scheduled for tonight, tomorrow night, or the night thereafter."

"That would seem logical, sir."

"Is there any pattern to the timing of the killings?"

"I don't understand what you mean," Houdain said.

"At what time of the night did the attacker usually strike?"

"We have no way of knowing that for sure, sir," the captain said. "Most were found the next day, and by then, the remains were quite cold and stiff. However, the fifth victim, the Pope's niece, was discovered during the second hour of the night, not long after she died—her corpus was still warm to the touch. She must have been murdered about sunset."

"Yes, I can confirm that," Doctor Martial said. He was a pudgy man of about sixty years, with a short, gray beard. "I was called to the scene immediately, and I can vouch that she didn't stiffen into the rigor mortis for at least another hour after I arrived."

"Also, we believe that several of the victims may have died somewhat later in the night," the officer said, "because we had witnesses who reported having passed the locations where the bodies were found during the early hours of the previous evening, and they reported seeing nothing at the time. At least one of these alleys was so narrow that someone walking there would have literally stumbled over the remains, if they'd been present then."

"Very well—I'd like to examine each of the death sites tomorrow, Houdain."

"Of course, sir."

"Now, tell me about the condition of the bodies when discovered," Master William said.

"But, sir, there are ladies present!" the officer said.

"In my youth, I labored on my father's farm," Mother Méraudine said. "Nothing that you can say will shock me. And Sister Sassica is our infirmarian and nurse; she's seen many sick and dying individuals over the years. She'll be my liaison for this investigation."

"But these poor women," Houdain said, "were butchered like pigs, cut up into pieces and strewn all over their final resting place. I've witnessed death in all its most gruesome forms, Father, and I tell you that these were the worst that I've ever seen. Several of my men refused to visit another such scene."

"Relate to me exactly what you found at each site," my master said.

I swallowed loudly. There were things here, depravities and horrors, that I didn't really want to know; but my illustrious master always insisted that I be present on such occasions.

"It's not enough, young Thaddæus," he'd tell me, "to appreciate the many good things of life. You must also know the depths to which a man can sink. You must find some way of resisting the evil, or it'll take you unawares one day, and you'll have nothing inside with which to fight it off."

He was right, of course, as he was in most things, but I didn't always realize this during my youth. His wisdom and essential goodness sometimes obscured the moral steel that bolstered his character, creating an impression of a weakness that simply didn't exist.

Houdain sighed before beginning. "It seemed to me that the body parts were, well, laid out in a certain way—different each time, mind you, but arranged in some pattern known only to the killer. Neither I nor my men could understand the message being given there. Doctor Martial can provide the medical details."

"The nuns had been raped, strangled, sliced, stabbed, and then cut apart with some very sharp implement, maybe a short sword or a butcher's knife," the physician said. "I found indications that some of the cuts were made by a serrated blade—but not always."

"Do either of you think that more than one individual was involved?" my master asked.

"We...," both men started to respond, and then Houdain took up the narrative again: "I found no such indication, sir. The scenes suggested—I saw several examples of what appeared to be the killer's footsteps marked in the spatters of blood at the scene—that only one person assaulted each woman. However, the doctor and I both noted that the shoe size of the killer differed in two instances. Also, minor differences in the ways in which the ladies were butchered seemed to match the variation in footwear."

"I saw the same thing, Father William," said Sister Sassica, a woman of perhaps thirty years. "When I prepared the bodies for burial—and I handled all but one—I noticed certain markings that were left by the killer."

"What kind of markings?" my master asked.

"On two of the corpses, the murderer etched a pyramid over and between the breasts of the victims, with the bottom points touching the teats; a third line dropped from the top of the pyramid to bisect the base. On the chests of the other two remains, the glyph cut into the bodies was a vertical line bisecting the breasts, with a horizontal line connecting to the top of the first line at a straight angle, left across the body until it ended above the nipple."

"Were there any other marks of note?"

"As the officer mentioned, the killer or killers had slashed and punctured the bodies indiscriminately, with no evident pattern. However, I discovered upon the person of each victim a square piece or pieces of bronze, impressed with a letter of the alphabet. These were stuffed into various apertures of the bodies."

"Do you still have these markers?"

"Yes, Father, I'll make certain you get them."

"Very good," Father William said. "Captain Houdain, do you have a map of where and when the victims were found?"

"No, sir, but I can certainly make one for you."

"Please do so. Sister, if you could bring me those metal pieces at our cottage…?"

"Yes, right away, Father," she said.

"We'll break for now. Thank you, everyone, for your help."

As we were leaving the Papal Palace, Houdain caught up with us, and handed my master a note. "I was asked to pass this along to you, sir," he said.

Father William opened the slip, glanced at the message, and

then frowned. "Captain, do you know why Father Seraphim was arrested?"

"He was, uh, confronted by one of the men posted to guard our visitors from the east, whilst leaving their quarters early this morning at the Abbey of Saint Junien. His papers had expired. Per our usual procedure, we incarcerate such individuals until their identities can be verified."

"I realize that this isn't your area of authority, Captain, but could you possibly take us there right away, and see if we can interview this man?"

"I can try, sir."

"Thank you," my teacher said.

* * * * * * *

THE DUNGEONS beneath the Rocher des Doms had been carved out of the rock by the secular princes who had once owned the fortress. We were led down a narrow, damp, winding pathway to the least secure section of the jail, in the upper portion of the complex.

"Father Seraphim" was housed with a dozen other reprobates awaiting examination for a series of minor offenses. Father William was able to secure a private interview without difficulty.

"What are you playing at here, Michael?" my master asked, when we were alone with the man. The force of his words crackled through the air like a roll of thunder. "What's your *real* reason for coming to Avignon?"

"I didn't lie to you, William," the head of the Franciscan Order said. "I did—and do—want your support for our enterprise, and I'm sorry that you can't give it. Perhaps you'll change your mind later.

"But, the truth is, I'm not alone. Traveling with me is Count Bavo von Indracht, the Emperor's representative, plus several guards. We've been charged by Ludwig with seeking support for the pope's deposition."

"Since when does the elected head of a religious body take directions from a secular leader, Michael? *Our* King is Jesus Christ."

"Yes, but we have to live in the real world, William," Cesena said. "I'm not anyone's puppet, but I do believe in exploring all the options available to us.

"The presence at the Papal Court of a delegation from the Patriarch of Constantinople was simply too good of an opportunity to miss. Some theologians and historians believe that the Ecumenical Patriarch has as much right to our respect and duty as the Pope, whom the easterners regard as merely the Patriarch of Rome and the Western Church. Isaias does provide us with a potential alternative should the center fail.

"John is expressing views that in the minds and hearts of many of us border on the heretical. When *our* elected leader goes mad, when he disavows the teachings of Jesus, what do we do then? We're rapidly reaching that point."

"Your actions here would be regarded as treasonous by the Pope—and also by many of the political leaders in the West. We can't afford to have our Order go the way of the Templars."

"We have a difference of opinion there," Father Michael said. "I have a responsibility to those who chose *me*—and I intend to honor it. Now, sir, can you get me out of here or not?"

Father William interceded with the captain of the prison guard, and vouched for the good character of "Father Seraphim," which gained him a new temporary passport for the Papal States, good for another month.

On our way down from the hill with Cesena, my master said: "You've forced me to lie for you, Michael. It won't happen again. Understand...old...friend?"

"Yes," he said, and we went our separate ways.

* * * * * * *

WE FOUND SISTER Sassica waiting for us at our cottage. She handed my master a set of eight small, roughly square bronze tokens. Each had a letter inscribed on one side—E, I, K, or S. An "I" and an "E" had been found on the body of the first victim, Sister Birina; an "E" on the body of Sister Rumona; an "I" and an "S" on the body of Sister Ernina; an "I" and an "E" on the body of Sister Astrée; and a "K" on the body of Sister Basilia. I thought that the shape of the "E" was odd—rounded on the left side—and said so.

"I have to admit, young Thaddæus," my master said, "that I'm puzzled by these...things. I sense some rough relationship between the pieces, but I don't know exactly what it is. I think we need to consult our Jewish friend again."

"A *Jew*?" Sister Sassica said, the despite evident on her frowning face. "Why would you *ever* consort with such heathens, Father?"

"Because they're men and women just like the rest of us, Sister, despite their different beliefs; also, they sometimes have knowledge about matters that the rest of us don't understand very well."

"Well, I certainly can't be a party to such things," she said, "so I'll take my leave of you now, if you please."

But Father William was still turning over the tokens in his hand, glaring at each as if waiting for them to speak. Alas, that they said not a word in reply!

* * * * * * *

WE VISITED MASTER Yehuda ben Sion at his home and shop in the Jewish Quarter, and I found him changed but little since our previous encounter earlier in the year.

"How good to see you again, Frère Occam!" he said. "And our young Pole—greetings, Thaddæus! You grow taller every time I see you. What treasures do you have for me this time?"

"What do you make of these, my friend?" my teacher said, putting the eight tokens in the shopkeeper's hand.

"Hmm," the old Jew said. "I wonder...." He wandered back into his workroom, motioning us to follow. The place was overflowing with clutter—implements of all kinds, manuscripts, jars of this and that and the other, and even a curious lizard with large eyes perched on a bush growing in a small cage, its prehensile claws clutching at the branches.

"What's this, sir?" I asked, pointing at the strange creature.

"'Ami' comes from Africa," the mage said. "They call it a *'chamaileon'* in Greek, or the 'small lion,' but of course it's a reptile, as you can see. It can change the color of its skin to hide in the background of its surroundings."

"Really?" I said.

"Truly, my son.

"Now, as to your little problem, gentlemen," the Jew said, "This is what I think." He pulled out a scale, and put the metal piece marked "K" on one side, and two of the tokens marked "I" on the other—and, *mirabile dictu*, they exactly balanced! "These are weights, marked with Greek numbers. 'E' means five units, 'I' ten, and 'K' twenty."

"What about the 'S'?" I asked.

"An obsolete letter called the 'digamma' or 'episemon'," he said. "It stands for the number six."

"Well, that tells us what they are," Father William said, "But not what they mean. Do you have any ideas on that subject, Master Yehuda?"

"Alas, I do not," he said.

"Then, we thank for your help," my teacher said.

And then we returned to our cottage.

* * * * * * *

THAT AFTERNOON, Officer Houdain brought Father William the diagram that he'd promised to prepare, and also took us on a tour of the five murder sites. They were all located in the poorer areas of Avignon—back alleys, narrow byways, or semi-abandoned shrines and other ruins.

"What were these women doing here?" I asked.

"All were acolytes running errands for their religious

houses," the captain said. "Some were taking food or medicine to those in need, while others were carrying messages from one abbey to another."

"Apprentices of all kinds"—and here Father William looked down at me and smiled crookedly—"are assigned many tasks that no one else wishes to handle."

"So I've noticed," I said.

"What I find curious," my master said, "is that these nuns showed no signs of having fought for their lives. They appeared to have accepted their killer right up to the point where he suddenly took control.

"This tells me that he was presentable, even respectable, perhaps well dressed, possibly wealthy or powerful, someone who was used to being followed or obeyed. Such men would not be challenged by young women of this age."

"But what was his game, sir?" Houdain asked. "What did he hope to accomplish by these senseless killings?"

"Perhaps just to demonstrate that he could, although I sense something else at work here, some underlying reason that we haven't fathomed yet. The Greek weights must have a meaning to the killer or killers—but what?"

"Maybe the very fact that they're Greek can tell us something, master," I said.

"A good point," he said. "Captain, when did the delegation from the Ecumenical Patriarch arrive?"

"Uh, I think it was about ten days before the Calends of September."

"Or perhaps four or five days before the first murder," Occam said. "How many men made the journey from Constantinople?"

"The party consists of three clergymen—Metropolitan Joasaph, Father Gennadios, and Bishop Bartholomaios—plus several secular aides, Master Julian and Master Kosmas. The guards that had protected them during their voyage were replaced at the border of the Papal States with men from our own troop."

"They're all staying at Saint Junien?"

"Yes, sir."

"Who among the Papal staff has a working knowledge of the Greek language?" my master asked.

"Well, uh, Bishop Écorchure is able to talk with them; he comes originally from Dalmatia, which has some commerce with the Empire, I understand. To help with the translation of documents, the Pope also brought in several priests from other locations—uh, Fathers Symmaque, Persée, and Glaucos. We had to provide papers for all three men."

"I'd like a list of these, if you please," Occam said, "with their backgrounds, ages, and current places of residence."

"I'll do what I can, sir," Houdain said, "but without actually interrogating these people, I doubt if I can find out all that much about them."

"Can I gain access to them?" my master asked.

"To the Papal staff, yes, but the head of the Greek delegation would have to give his permission for you to interview any of his people. They're out of our jurisdiction."

"There must be a way."

Captain Houdain left us then. Father William was still ruminating on the problem when we stopped at an inn to buy ourselves a simple meal of stewed lamb, freshly baked bread, and some apples that had been cooked and sweetened with sugar. I particularly enjoyed the latter.

"You can still manage such things without consequences," my master said. "I, on the other hand…." He patted his small round tummy.

We finished the rest of our meal in silence, thinking our own thoughts about what we'd been told and seen that day. I couldn't put the pictures of the blood-stained cobbles out of my mind.

"So what do we do now, Master?" I finally asked.

He looked very old for a brief moment. "There's naught to do but wait," he said. "We wait for the next murder, and hope that our sixth victim tells us something more than the rest."

* * * * * * *

BUT ONCE WE'D returned to our cottage, we waited and waited—and still nothing happened! Finally, Father William suggested that we head off to bed, and I was sound asleep, being chased around the cottage by a mad killer, when the pounding began. I rolled out of my blanket, pulled on my shift, and headed for the door.

"Captain Houdain," I said, inviting the man in. The officer's face was even grimmer than usual. My master was already awake and ready to receive the bad news.

"It's one of our own this time," he said, "one of the men on patrol. He was cut down perhaps a block from where the first killing took place. They found him when he failed to report."

Houdain explained that he'd set up a rotating series of patrols through the poorer sections of Avignon that had been targeted before and were likely to be targeted in the future. Each man was assigned a specific area and specific route, with regular meetings scheduled at the main junctions. When one of the patrolmen failed to appear, the survivor raised the alarm, and all the others converged on the area. The body of the missing man was soon found.

"Per your orders, Father William, the scene and the body parts have been left untouched. He couldn't have been killed much more than an hour ago at most, around moonrise."

"Moonrise?" my master asked. He paused for a moment, and then asked: "The body of the pope's niece, Sister Basilia, was found precisely when?"

"Six days ago, about two hours into the night," Houdain said.

"Six days ago was the full moon, which rose precisely at sunset. These murders are being scheduled by the phases of the moon! Today is the onset of the third quarter."

"What does it all mean, Master?" I asked.

"I wish that I knew, Thaddæus. Now, gather your pack of implements, and your courage, and let's go see what the killer has left us this time."

* * * * * * *

THE JUDGMENT OF THE GODS | 109

It took us ten minutes to reach the scene of the current crime in the Colbert District, the place where Sister Rumona had also been murdered. When we entered Crapaud Alley, or the Place of the Toad, I nearly lost my dinner. The smell of fresh blood permeated the atmosphere.

Doctor Martial was waiting for us, as was Sister Sassica.

"Why have *you* come?" my master asked the nun.

"I think they assumed that the victim would again be a woman, and so I was called out right away. I can still be useful, however, since I helped clean and lay out most of the previous bodies. The blood and guts don't bother me."

"Very well. Before we proceed, I want all of you to stand back and take in the scene before you." The narrow alleyway was brightly illuminated on both sides (front and rear) with torches held high by the guards. "What happened here, and in what order?"

"Well, Father," Sister Sassica said, "once again it appears that the victim offered very little resistance to the killer. The footprints directly behind the body suggest that the guard turned his back on his assailant, leaving himself defenseless."

"I agree," Captain Houdain said.

"As do I," my master said. "Now, Doctor, you may begin your examination. Try to disturb the remains as little as possible."

The physician picked up the guard's severed head and peered closely at the shredded flesh of his neck. "Yesss, there are signs of strangulation, as before. You can see the cord marks if you look closely." He held the bloodied skull up to us.

"Can you tell whether he was garroted from the front or the rear?" Father William asked.

"Oh, definitely from the rear. The marks are higher at the back. All of the remaining injuries are *post mortem*. I think they were accomplished with a short sword of some kind—and done very hurriedly. See here—one of the arms has been hacked—but not quite all the way through. Note the striking mark on the shattered cobble underneath.

"And, what's this? Yes, there's another one of those metal

pieces forced up the man's right nostril." He pulled it out, wiped it on his cloak, and handed it to Father William.

"An 'M,'" my teacher said. "The Greek letter signifying the number forty. This one was worth more than the rest, perhaps due to his status as a soldier or to the risks that the killer took when he attacked him. But forty...what? What kind of game is being played with these innocents?

"We're going to need something special to help elucidate this puzzle. The speculum, if you would, please, Thaddæus, and the little fork, the furcilla. All of you save Sister Sassica, Doctor Martial, and Captain Houdain must withdraw from the scene temporarily. You three may remain to hold the torches, but stand back a few paces, please."

The guards hastened to depart, stopping just beyond the next street corners on either side.

Meanwhile, I removed the magical implements from their carrying pack, and sat on the filthy stones well away from the pools of blood. I crossed my legs, and held the supernally polished mirror between my hands. When my teacher came over, he took the furcilla, and we were ready.

Soon I had the metal circle spinning in front of me, reflecting the light from the three torches in an odd array of brilliant flashes—red and yellow and orange.

I focused my efforts on recreating what had just happened here—the slaughter of an unsuspecting and essentially defenseless man. Slowly, the images began coming together, and my master stepped behind me to review the unfolding drama. We saw the guard leading a hooded man down the alley, before being suddenly garroted from behind. He struggled for a moment, but the strong arms of his assailant were unrelenting. Then he dropped his torch to the ground, but it remained lit.

"Ah," my master said, and I saw what he meant. Although the killer's face remained in shadow throughout, perhaps through a magically-induced mask, we could see a ruby ring that adorned the index finger of his left hand. Even in the dim, flickering light, it remained quite visible.

THE JUDGMENT OF THE GODS | 111

Once the guard was dead, the assailant pulled a short sword from under his cape, and began hacking at the body with a frenzy that bordered almost on joy—if murderers can be said to feel such emotions.

While the killer was completing his butchery, Father William carefully brought the furcilla closer to the spinning metal mirror, and symbolically stabbed the assailant through his heart.

"Ahhh!" the man in the speculum said. He straightened abruptly, as if he'd been stung by a large bee, and quickly looked around—but saw nothing, for truth be told, the darkness both literal and figurative had grown as the victim's torch had diminished.

"*Fiat lux!*" we heard the killer say, and his weapon lit up, casting long shadows down both stretches of the alleyway. But again, he saw nothing, for, of course, we were not really there.

"*Where* is the connection?" I heard my master murmur to himself, and stabbed the assailant again with the furcilla.

Abruptly, the image of the alley drained away from the speculum, and was replaced by the rapidly growing tableau of a hooded man (presumably the same one) sitting in front of a game board, facing an opponent equally enshrouded. The Hooded One was playing the black pieces in the sit-down tourney called *échecs*, or sometimes just "knights." His challenger employed the crimson-hued men.

The killer moved a black bishop to take a red knight, his jeweled ring flashing in the light, and added it to a row that included two *pions*—the most minor pieces on the board, and a stack of the bronze weights. He handed one of the metal pieces across the board, and nodded to the other that it was his turn to play.

Then the Hooded One looked up and said something that we couldn't hear, because both men abruptly stood up and waved their hands in a joint incantation that immediately cut off our access.

"What was *that*?" Sister Sassica asked, her voice tremulous.

"Some of the answer, I think," said Father William, "but not one that Pope John will ever accept. In truth, Sister, I'm not sure if even *I* accept it."

* * * * * * *

WE RETURNED HOME, where we captured a few hours of much-needed rest. In the morning, Father William dispatched messages to Captain Houdain, Sister Sassica, and "Father Seraphim" to meet us there in the first hour of the afternoon.

"Gentlemen and lady," my master said, when all had arrived and seated themselves in the main room of our cottage, "We find ourselves in the curious situation of knowing *how* these crimes were committed, at least physically, but not the names of the perpetrators." He then summarized each of the steps that we'd taken to date.

"The images that we saw in the speculum tell me that two individuals are involved, and that they're playing a very dangerous game indeed, manipulating the counters on the board ultimately to result in the deaths of innocent victims. The spilling of real blood is the essential and binding component of what must certainly be a very dark spell, designed to give one of the players some significant advantage at the conclusion of the game.

"The presence in Avignon of a delegation from the Ecumenical Patriarch cannot be accidental. At stake is a possible merging of two divided ecclesiastical bodies, East and West, and all of the potential political and religious consequences deriving therefrom. If this overture fails, it could ultimately mean the end of a weakened Eastern Empire, which guards the gateway into Europe—but an increase in the power and influence of the Eastern Church. If it succeeds, the Pope, who has recently been under fire from all quarters, will be greatly bolstered.

"Either way, the stakes are high enough that both sides—or at least some individuals from each party—have decided to wager everything on a gamble with the Devil.

"I don't have to tell you that those involved are damned, now

THE JUDGMENT OF THE GODS | 113

and for all eternity. What they're doing is an abomination of what our Christian religion represents. I can't believe that Pope John and Patriarch Isaias are directly involved, that the corruption has reached so high. But in any case, before we can take steps against the killers, we must first identify them."

There was a long silence thereafter, as everyone tried to think of something to say. They were as appalled as I by what Father William had described.

"The game was *échecs*?" "Father Seraphim" said.

"Yes. They were playing red and black counters. The murderer took a crimson knight, which corresponded symbolically to Captain Houdain's patrolman—and hence was worth forty units in the game, more than any other piece sacrificed thus far. The object must be to take as many of the opponent's men as possible—and not just to mate the king."

"Well," Cesena continued, "I know that Father Gennadios fancies himself a master of the game. He told me that it was the one thing that alleviated his boredom during the long trip from Constantinople to Avignon; but that none of his party had provided him with much of a challenge, and he was forced to find better players scattered along the route."

"So, he's a definite possibility. That would explain the Greek letter Gamma carved on two of the victims' chests."

"*Three* victims," Sister Sassica said. "The man who was murdered last night also bore such a mark."

"I stand corrected," my teacher said. "So, if he's the Greek king in this game, who represents the other side?"

"Count von Indracht," "Seraphim" said, "once offered to play me a game, but I was forced to tell him that, while I know the moves and the theory, I don't think strategically, which makes me a very poor gamester."

"What does the Count's name mean?" Father William asked.

Cesena knew many different languages, from his native Italian to French to Latin to German, which made him a good representative of his Order at international meetings. "Well," he said, "There are several possible cognates. '*Drache*' means 'dragon,' and '*Direktor*' means 'director.' I've heard it said that he fancies himself as a possible candidate as Emperor Ludwig's successor."

"The Greek monogram carved on the other victims' chests was a delta-iota, 'D'-'I' in our alphabet, which could stand for '*Direktor*', or as an 'I'-'D' for 'In-Dracht'. So, he's a candidate for the crimson tide.

"But, what do these men gain by risking their souls? What are the stakes if each of them wins?"

"The Byzantine Emperor, Andronikos II, is an old man," "Father Seraphim" said. "He was the one who repudiated the last union between the churches of Rome and Constantinople, when he first came to the throne forty years ago. Now his realm is involved in a civil war being waged against him by his grandson and namesake, Andronikos III, and he's also engaged in a longstanding war with the Turkish hordes in Asia Minor. In the end, he will lose both of those conflicts, I believe.

"His grandson is looking for any advantage that he can bring to bear. Since the old man opposes the union between East and West, the younger one now favors it. His representative here, I think, is young Gennadios, who's made no secret of his impatience with both the Metropolitan and the Patriarch, and of his ambition to replace both in due course. If he wins, his patron wins, and the two old men are deposed. Avignon is a very long way from Constantinople, and religious autonomy under the Pope is quite acceptable—for a few years, at least."

"And, on the other side?" my master said.

"If Count von Indracht prevails, Pope John's attempt to reach out to the East is discredited, the discontent grows among the clergy, cardinals, and temporal rulers, and the possibility of the pontiff being deposed and replaced with a partisan of Ludwig is greatly advanced. Ludwig could care less whether the Eastern Empire—or Eastern Church—falls. He wants his freedom from the Western Church to rule as he pleases, without interference. The popes, he's now saying, have abandoned Rome, their pastoral home, and have therefore become illegitimate successors to Saint Peter, since all the canons and precedents tie bishops and archbishops directly to their sees. Even titular bishops are given titular sees. And for Indracht, of course, a win would also advance his power base for a chance at being elected Emperor when Ludwig dies."

"Yes, all of that makes good political sense."

"What about the link to the phases of the moon, sir?" I asked. "Why is that necessary?"

"In the dark arts, the moon can be a huge source of power, waxing and waning through its four phases in a predictable progress that provides cold but reliable energy to those who can tap its leys—and are willing to pay the price. Once locked into the cycle, the players must complete their game to its final destination, repaying their draws in blood—or be destroyed by the very æther that they've accessed. It's a very dangerous enterprise, very risky to all involved, but those who survive can gain an immense control of elemental forces. That's why we must stop this exercise before it proceeds any further. If we've identified the players correctly, how do we discredit them and bring this game to an end?"

"Well, sir, I couldn't arrest the Count, even if you could prove his guilt—he's outside my jurisdiction, as is that Greekish fellow," said Captain Houdain.

"You're right," Father William said. "We're not going to see conventional justice take its course here, my friends. And I won't countenance direct physical violence, even if it's justified. No, we must devise a plan that will work in some other fashion. The next murder will take place during the new moon, seven days from now, when the stakes are at their highest. We have until then."

After much discussion that led nowhere, we shared a simple meal of meat and bread and cheese, and then the others went their separate ways, sworn to secrecy—"For," as Father William emphasized, "if our suspicions became known to the perpetrators, they could advance their agenda very quickly, and attempt to push the contest to its extreme before any of us—or them—

are ready for it."

* * * * * * *

A WEEK LATER, we *were* ready.

"Are you certain that you want to go through with this?" my master asked Sister Sassica. "It's likely to be a very dangerous gambit. There's no shame in backing out."

"If my actions will save a life, then it's worth the risk," she said. "I knew two of the women who were killed, Father. They were good and decent people, devoted to their vocation and to a life of contemplation and aid to the poor. They didn't deserve to have their time on earth cut short in this brutal fashion."

"Then we'll proceed," he said.

We'd established a base in a house in the Bélon District, near to the small, half-ruined fountain where the third victim, Sister Ernina, had been found. Captain Houdain had also hidden a number of his men wherever he could in the immediate vicinity, all of them carrying whistles to call for help, if needed.

I prepared the speculum, the furcilla, and caduceus. Then Officer Houdain, "Father Seraphim," Sister Sassica, Father William, and I prayed that the Lord God would give us strength to fight the Evil One and his earthly minions.

After blessing the nun with holy water, my master gave her a crucifix containing a sliver of the true cross to wear 'round her neck, and wished her well. Now, all we could do was wait.

She began her trek two hours before dawn, with only the stars and her own torch to guide her. She followed a circuit that remained close to all of the emplacements where our guards were waiting, walking back and forth just a few blocks in one direction, before turning and coming back the other way. She carried a bag under one arm.

I activated the metal mirror, but tuned to the audio portion only, hoping to avoid being noticed by the two players. Finally, I heard a man say, "Your move," and his opponent respond, "Bishop takes pawn."

"It's begun!" I hissed to the others, keeping control of the mirror, while Father William took the furcilla, and "Father Seraphim" the caduceus. We gathered around the one window, trying to pierce the impenetrable blackness.

Suddenly, Captain Houdain said, "A torch!"—but no one could tell whether this was the nun, her possible assailant, or someone else approaching. As the light drew nearer, I could gradually distinguish Sister Sassica's pale features beneath the flickering light.

Then Father William said, "He comes!" and I turned to see another torch-bearer approaching our site from the opposite direction. This was very strange, because no one had been there just a moment earlier.

"Excuse me, please," I heard the man say to the nun, "I appear to be lost. Do you know the way to Saint-Boisile's?"

"It's just a few blocks from here," Sassica said.

"I am s-strange in this town," he said, emphasizing his foreign accent, "and I would appreciate being shown the way, if you could help."

"It's really quite easy to find," she said. "Just turn around and continue until you reach the second cross-street, then head right. You'll find it a short distance up the hill to your left."

"Please, could you show me?"

"I'm running very late," she said. "But, if you insist, I'll follow you back the other way."

"But...."

Then Sassica thrust her torch between them, illuminating the area under his hood, and she immediately drew back in fear and horror. "Fiend of Hell, what *are* you?" she asked. "You have no face!"

"I need no face to kill," he said, but the fire kept him back, and we rushed out of the house into the alleyway behind her. Houdain blew a whistle, and we heard his men emerging from their holes to join us front and rear.

The trapped killer looked around wildly, but there was no place to run, no shadow in which to hide. The light grew as more torches were added to the confined space, and I held the speculum up to where it reflected the assailant's visage back to him.

"Ahhh!" I heard him say, trying to avoid looking at the nothingness that constituted his soul.

"What's happening?" a voice asked from a distance, but the trapped one could not respond.

The killer tried dashing around our small group, but Father William spoke a word under his breath, and his furcilla grew to become a furca, a large, two-pronged pitchfork glowing with golden radiant energy that blocked the man's exit.

Then Father Michael, who was known to most of these people only as "Father Seraphim," stepped forward around the woman, and banged the caduceus on the cobblestones, proclaiming, "Go back!" The killer's own torch flared high, setting the man's hood on fire, and he began screaming as the self-inflicted pyre quickly consumed him from the top to the bottom, leaving nothing on the soiled pavement but a pile of foul-smelling, decaying ash.

"What *was* that?" Captain Houdain asked.

"A psychic projection," my master said. "In one sense, there was nothing actually present other than the warped spirit of someone who was using otherworldly powers for base ends; but since the spirit and the flesh are inextricably linked, his spiritual death has probably also had its physical counterpart. As I told you, great energies were being manipulated here, and the slightest loss of control under such circumstances can be disastrous to the players."

"And what of the other killer?" Sister Sassica asked.

"They were both tied to the spell that they created together, and thus both will suffer the consequences of their dabbling in the black arts. There's never a good ending to this tale. Some men—some women as well—just don't seem to understand the price that they have to pay for the power that they crave so much.

"But God knows, and it's to Him—and to their victims—that these two will now have to justify their actions."

"When will *we* know, Father?"

"Tomorrow, my child. We'll hear tomorrow what has happened to these men—but none of us will respond to it, because no one would believe us if we did."

* * * * * * *

THE NEXT DAY, the news spread throughout the town of the strange deaths of Father Gennadios and Count von Indracht, who were completely consumed with flames whilst playing chess late at night.

The talks between the representatives of the Pope and the Ecumenical Patriarch continued for another month, but ultimately reached no agreement, and the good Metropolitan then returned to Constantinople to make his report, promising to reappear in the spring.

And Father William and I met again with Papa John at the Palais des Papes a week after the strange passings of the Greek priest and the representative of Emperor Ludwig.

"Have you found the killer of my great-niece?" the pontiff asked, leaning forward on his throne. His face was lined, and a tic had developed on the left side of his mouth.

"We have, Holiness," my teacher said.

"Who was it?"

"There are some things that a leader should not know," Father William said.

The pope looked around the room at his attendants, including Bishop Écorchure, waved his right hand, and said, "Leave us! Leave us immediately, all of you save the priest and his acolyte."

When we were alone with John, he said: "What you say is very true, Occam, but it's also true that a man must take care of his own. Sister Basilia was one of mine, and I owe this to her memory. I don't need to know the specific circumstances, but I must ask you again, as one man to another: *who was it?*"

"Father Gennadios and Count von Indracht."

"Ah." It was a sigh as well as an exaltation of sorrow. "Ahhh," he said again. "I did wonder when I heard the news. I have lived

120 | ROBERT REGINALD

too long, I think, to see my younger kin be dragged down by fiends such as these.

"Still, the killers have been punished, and I did not have to emerge from the shadows to do this thing."

"They did it to themselves," Father William said. "Or rather, God settled their accounts."

"He settles all of our accounts in the end," Pope John said. "I know that you think very little of me, Occam, but I've done the best that I could to maintain the ship of the church on a even keel, not veering too far to the right or to the left, and trying to keep the crew and passengers happy—or at least satisfied.

"I thought once that attaining this office was the greatest achievement of my life, and now I see that it was the least. Any fool can be elected to this chair. Very few, however, rest in it comfortably. I've become a prisoner of my ambition. Once I had all the time in the world, time to think, to plan, to glorify God in all His works. And now—now, I have no time left at all.

"You've done me a great service, Occam. In return, I grant you the life of your friend, Michael de Cesena. He has three days in which to leave my temporal realm. If he's still here after that time, I *will* have him arrested and tried.

"Now, leave me alone, both of you!"

* * * * * * *

WE SOUGHT OUT the head of the Franciscan Order immediately, and gave him the Pope's warning.

"I would heed his advice," my master told his friend.

"I'll leave first thing in the morning," Cesena said. "I haven't given up the idea of replacing that old goat with someone younger, but we need a better plan to accomplish the task."

"Yes, you do," Father William said. "I wish you Godspeed, Michael."

"And to you, my brother in Christ. And to you."

Breinigsville, PA USA
30 January 2011

254380BV00001B/37/P